ADVANCE PRAISE

"As a twenty-six-year leader at the Disney Company, people often ask me the secret to Disney's mystical customer experience. The truth is it's all about creating a culture of extraordinary customer service, and Charles Ryan Minton is sharing his expertise in his fantastic new book *Thanks for Coming in Today*. I've worked with Ryan and can say from personal experience that he knows his stuff. He walks the talk and knows how to lead teams to do the same. This is not some empty academic theory. I encourage you to buy a copy for every member of your team to learn his behind-the-scenes secrets to world-class excellence...before your competition does!"

—MARK DAVID JONES, PRESIDENT, SMALL WORLD ALLIANCE AND FORMER DISNEY EXECUTIVE

"For years, my management team has had the same three great customer service books as required reading. I have not found a fourth book (and I've read them all) worthy of adding as mandatory reading for our team until now! I will be putting *Thanks for Coming in Today* in the hands of every one of my team members. It's that good. This is a winner!"

—MIKE HAMILTON, FRANCHISEE, CHIEF OPERATING OFFICER, PLANET FITNESS MIDWEST

"*Creating an outstanding and memorable customer experience is the most important element of running a successful business. Most managers err by looking at customer service as a protocol issue. Charles Ryan Minton sees phenomenal customer service as a natural extension of a phenomenal employee culture. In Ryan's book Thanks for Coming in Today, service industry leaders will find low-cost, easy-to-implement tools and strategies that will begin to elevate and transform their customer experience immediately.*"

—JANE GROTE ABELL, CHAIRWOMAN OF THE BOARD, DONATOS PIZZA, AND FEATURED IN CBS'S *UNDERCOVER BOSS*

"*The foundation of any great company, organization, or nonprofit lies within their human capital. Investing in your employees and creating a space where they feel heard, empowered, respected, and engaged naturally feeds into how they interact with your visitors or customers. At the Cincinnati Zoo & Botanical Garden, we aim to create the best visitor experience in the nation, and we get there through investing heavily in the relationships we build with our frontline team. When we do that well, you can see the returns on that investment through the trickle-down effect of happier employees, more engaged visitors and members, and huge returns in our revenue stream.*

"*In his book Thanks for Coming in Today, Charles Ryan Minton does a remarkable job of explaining, down to the nuts and bolts, how to be the best leader you can be in the visitor experience space and how to get the best out of your employees. If you fully embrace the ideas and concepts that Ryan so artfully lays out, you will see success in your brand and business. Secondarily and maybe more importantly, you will walk away with stronger relationships and will be building a better community."*

—RHIANNON HOEWELER, VICE PRESIDENT OF
VISITOR EXPERIENCE, STRATEGY AND FUN,
CINCINNATI ZOO & BOTANICAL GARDEN

"Charles Ryan Minton's new book Thanks for Coming in Today is a gem for service-excellence tactics and foundational experience ideas. Every service example he details in each chapter can be embraced and put into action in any industry from hospitality to healthcare. This is a must-read for all customer-, guest-, and patient-experience leaders!"

—JENNIFER JASMINE E. ARFAA, PHD, CHIEF
EXPERIENCE OFFICER AND VICE PRESIDENT
OF PATIENT EXPERIENCE, UC HEALTH

"At Jaguar and Land Rover, we understand that our customers expect more than just a quality product. Luxury brands like ours have to deliver superior customer service. Charles Ryan Minton tailored content and a presentation that was relevant for our brand and gave actionable information we could implement to elevate our customer experience. I highly recommend working with Ryan!"

—RICHARD ALLEN, VICE PRESIDENT AND
GENERAL MANAGER, JAGUAR LAND ROVER

"*Often a forgotten art, Charles Ryan Minton conveys, through his extensive professional education and experiences, how to master customer service in today's changing marketplace. Ryan presents key core concepts in an understandable and easy-to-implement format. A must for anyone looking to enhance their customer experience.*"

—MARK HECQUET, EXECUTIVE DIRECTOR, BUTLER COUNTY VISITORS BUREAU

"*With a unique perspective—advancing from the front desk to general manager while employed by some of the world's largest hotel brands and high-profile companies—Charles Ryan Minton recognizes that an exceptional leader is one who knows the way, goes the way, and shows the way. Ryan shares the special qualities of being that exceptional leader to both customers and employees, which is synonymous with becoming yourself. Holding yourself to a higher standard is key to providing an unforgettable customer experience. It is one of many insightful learning opportunities Ryan offers to his readers.*"

—JOE HINSON, PRESIDENT AND CEO, WEST CHESTER LIBERTY CHAMBER ALLIANCE

THANKS FOR COMING IN TODAY

CHARLES RYAN MINTON

Thanks

for

Coming in
Today

CREATING A CULTURE WHERE EMPLOYEES
THRIVE AND CUSTOMER SERVICE IS ALIVE

LIONCREST
PUBLISHING

THANKS FOR COMING IN TODAY

Creating a Culture Where Employees Thrive
& Customer Service Is Alive

ISBN   978-1-5445-1208-2 *Hardcover*

978-1-5445-1207-5 *Paperback*

978-1-5445-1206-8 *Ebook*

To my wife, Geetha. Thank you for always being my number one fan.

In memory of Jason Fuller.

Contents

Introduction

―――

When I took over as the general manager of a suburban Marriott in Cincinnati, Ohio, the hotel was doing okay. Still, as with most service industry businesses, there was room for improvement. Specifically, there was room to bump up the hotel's customer service scores.

I came in to the job understanding that the only way this particular hotel was going to compete with the top Marriotts in North America was by improving its service. I love my hotel, but let's be honest—few people are clamoring to luxuriate in Ohio's gray winter weather or to indulge in the chain restaurants that surround the hotel. Great service was really the only viable way to set ourselves apart from competitors and establish our hotel as *the* obvious choice.

When I arrived, this particular Marriott was providing

good service, but it wasn't memorable service. In a business like this—or any service industry business, for that matter—good service won't cut it. As with many other customer-facing companies, hotels live and die by customer service surveys. This hotel was consistently receiving an average score of eight out of a possible ten. This might sound good enough, but as far as Marriott is concerned, an eight or lower may as well be a zero.

It was my job to change that. So I did. I tweaked the hotel's service culture by using the tools and strategies we'll discuss in the pages to come. Underlying all of this was the philosophy that if employees weren't having a great experience working for us, customers wouldn't have a great experience staying with us.

As the culture shifted, so did our scores. I watched as our customer rankings went up from sevens and eights to consistently landing in the nine or ten range. Then something incredible happened. Our hotel began to consistently crack the top ten of Marriott's ongoing ranking of its 360-plus full-service hotels. We even beat out destination locations. That's right, this Cincinnati Marriott became a heavy hitter.

If we can do it, you can do it. I'm going to show you how.

FROM GOOD TO GREAT

The strategies I employed to make this Marriott successful aren't rocket science. In fact, I've used these same strategies at every service industry company I've managed over the years. Without fail, employee engagement and customer satisfaction both drastically improve. It's simply a matter of resetting expectations among all levels and ensuring those expectations are met on a daily basis. This very much includes raising the bar and resetting your employees' expectations of you and the type of support they can count on receiving.

Most of all, I believe in empowering my employees. I let them know on a regular basis that what they do matters. I let them know *they* matter. I empower them to do what they feel needs to be done to make a positive impression on guests and to take care of problems when they arise without delay.

What I've learned over the years, both at this Marriott and in my other leadership positions within the service industry, is that it doesn't take as much as you might think to shift a culture. It doesn't take much to empower employees and allow them to thrive. It also doesn't take as much as you might think for employees to pass this feeling of genuine appreciation on to guests. All of this boils down to taking small but consistent measures. It's a matter of letting everyone—employees and customers alike—know that you are glad they're there. That you're thankful they made the choice to join you.

Whether you are working at a business that currently falls at a three or at a ten in service ratings, there's always room for improvement. There are always inroads that will make employees feel more empowered and customers feel more appreciated. No business is perfect. Wherever you currently land on the spectrum, I'm willing to bet that there are little things you can do to make your team enjoy coming to work a little bit more and, by extension, to make your guests even happier they chose your establishment out of all the options at their disposal.

Another benefit to all of this is that in leading this sort of culture, *you* will have a more enriching and self-affirming professional experience. It's hard not to love your job when everyone around you is empowered and satisfied.

Not only that, but it will make your job easier. When your front line is allowed to take care of problems as they arise and—even better—doing such a stellar job that fewer problems crop up in the first place, you are able to be more effective in other areas of your job. You have time to look at the big picture and move the dial in new ways. No one wants to spend their days putting out fires and responding to upset or unsatisfied customers.

START HERE

Since you're reading this book, chances are you're looking for ways to step up your customer service game, whether that means a sweeping overhaul or tiny tweaks here and there. Perhaps you want to move the needle a little bit closer to building your reputation as a great service provider *and* a great place to work.

The strategies you'll find within these pages are equally possible to roll out whether you're a mom-and-pop shop, a franchise, or an international chain. While this book is written with the service industry in mind, these principles will also work to great effect in any customer-facing business (which, when you think about it, is really all businesses).

I'm going to teach you how to level up by implementing some immediate, low-cost solutions that will transform your entire culture to a customer-centric enterprise from top to bottom. I'm willing to bet that accomplishing this will be far easier and less intimidating than you think. It also won't bust your budget. In fact, it won't even impact your budget, aside from increasing your bottom line as you bolster customer loyalty and garner the type of reviews that make you irresistible to new customers.

By the time you finish implementing these strategies, you will see a noticeable improvement in both customer service and customer experience. While there is some overlap in these terms, for the purposes of orienting ourselves, *customer service* refers to the rote tasks of taking care of customers—answering the phone, taking an order, checking someone in, or providing any type of concrete service.

Customer service happens as an action in the moment. *Customer experience* looks at the big picture. It is the sum of all service points that cumulatively amount to a customer's journey through your establishment and your brand, whether that ultimately amounts to a few minutes or several days. A customer's experience begins from the moment they see an advertisement about you or visit your website, continues through the duration of time they spend at your establishment, and includes any follow-up emails or other communication they might receive from you.

Customer service isn't enough in and of itself. Yes, your service should be friendly and proficient, but you can think of customer service as the assembly line of the service industry. The heart is in customer experience. Creating a stellar experience is critical. According to the 2017 Microsoft State of Global Customer Service, 59 percent of US customers have stopped doing business with a brand due to poor customer service.

It is through customer experience that clients can connect to and build a relationship with your business. To be memorable, you have to create an incredible experience. As you'll soon see, this is entirely possible regardless of where you're starting from today.

NICE TO MEET YOU

Since the age of fifteen, I have worked exclusively in the service industry. You name it, I've done it, including everything from my first job at a theme park to white-glove private aviation to serving as a general manager at a top-rated property of the largest hotel company in the world. I've worked my way up through multiple world-wide brands, including the three biggest international hotel chains. I've done it all, from being the low man on the totem pole to managing a large staff.

In that time, I've moved hotels from the bottom 20 to 25 percent of the brand to the top. I have increased employee engagement scores from 70 percent to 90 percent. The Marriott I mentioned earlier was the only hotel named on the *Cincinnati Business Courier's* list of best places to work. I was cited as "A Great Leader Under 40" in *Lead* magazine and named Business Person of the Year by the West Chester Liberty Chamber Alliance.

But all of this doesn't speak to what I strongly feel is my greatest accomplishment of all: I cultivate environments that not only do my employees and guests love stepping into every day, but so do I.

THE ONLY COST OF GREAT CUSTOMER SERVICE IS YOU

Remember how I told you about that Marriott that I turned around? It's worth underscoring the point that our rise to the top 5 percent of Marriotts in North America was solely based on our improved customer service and dedication to hospitality.

Situated on a highway exit, with three-fourths of the rooms facing the interstate and a giant electrical tower, this hotel wasn't exactly the sort of place people were booking for its exotic location or serene view. We didn't have a spa or any special amenities. It was just your basic full-service Marriott in suburban Ohio.

Not only that, but we had factors actively working *against* us. The hotel was undergoing a multi-million-dollar renovation at the time. This meant the lobby was blown to pieces and our customers were lulled by the dulcet sound of jackhammers. If you imagine yourself as a guest in this situation, it's probably no surprise to hear that hotel rankings generally dip during renovations. They certainly don't rise.

We were competing with Marriott properties in Arizona,

on the beaches of Florida and California, anywhere else you can imagine from East to West Coast, and throughout Canada and Mexico. Still, we came out on top.

I mention this one more time before we dig in because it proves that no matter what you're starting with, you can make your business's customer experience a great one. Too often, we focus on amenities and upgrades when we're looking to improve customer service. Don't get me wrong—all of these things are wonderful to have. But you don't need them to be great. At the end of the day, all you need is dedication to creating a culture in which employees can thrive and an unwavering focus on providing customer service that can't be beat. No extra expense or upgrades necessary.

PART ONE

Create a Culture of Success

CHAPTER ONE

Thanks for Coming in Today

———

When I was the front desk manager at a Marriott, I worked with a young man named Jason who was a hospitality student at a local university. Jason was one of those people who lit up the room. He was genuinely excited about people and wanted everyone around him to be happy and feel appreciated. I always wished that I could bottle up Jason's sunny personality, charisma, and high energy level, and sprinkle them over my entire team.

In his own way, that's exactly what Jason did.

As the department manager, I arrived at work before Jason every day. Nonetheless, as soon as he got to work every morning, Jason would immediately seek me out, look me directly in the eyes, and give me a hearty handshake. "Thanks for coming in today, Ryan," he would say, with all of the sincerity in the world. It was simultaneously funny and deeply endearing. After all, I was Jason's manager. I should be thanking *him* for coming in every day.

I wasn't the only one Jason greeted this way. As the day wore on, Jason greeted every single person he encountered—employees and guests alike—in the exact same manner.

Time went by, and Jason moved up the ranks. Without exception, Jason continued to greet everyone who crossed his path in his now-signature manner.

One of the worst phone calls I've ever received is the one that came in around 3:00 a.m. from Jason's fiancée. She was crying, so at first, it was difficult to understand what she was telling me. Then I understood: Jason had been killed in a car accident. The entire hotel staff was devastated. Jason was special. He was irreplaceable.

As a way of honoring Jason, I made a point of carrying on his tradition and greeting everyone just as he had. From there on out, I began every day by seeking out every employee and any guests I encountered along the way to give them a hearty handshake and look them in the eye as I said, "Thanks for coming in today."

After a while, I left the Marriott where Jason and I had worked together for another job. I took Jason's greeting with me. No matter where I worked after that, I carried on Jason's tradition of thanking everyone I met for coming in today. After a while, I didn't even realize I was doing it anymore. This little part of Jason became embedded in me.

At first, some of the staff I managed thought I was being sarcastic. "Of course I'm here. I'm working today," they would respond.

"No, really," I would explain. "I *genuinely* appreciate you coming in today. You have a choice about whether or not to come to work every single morning. When you don't, it impacts everything. It impacts your coworkers, it impacts customers, and it impacts the bottom line. I am so thankful that you came in today."

After a while, I realized that Jason's habit was contagious. Just like I had picked up the greeting from him, my employees picked it up from me. Over the years, it's become almost like a game, with staff members making a point of seeking me out before I could get to them. "Thanks for coming in today, Ryan!" they say, with a big smile and a handshake. Many times, when I run into former employees, they tell me, "As simple as it is, I really miss you shaking my hand and thanking me for coming in every day."

For as silly as this practice might sound, I can attest to the fact that every single time Jason thanked me for coming in, I felt like I mattered. I want my employees to feel that way too. In fact, it's critical that my employees feel that way. Employees who feel like they matter make customers feel like they matter.

THE CUSTOMER EXPERIENCE CLIMATE TODAY

Now more than ever, one of the primary ways companies in the service industry—and every industry, for that matter—differentiate themselves is through memorable customer service. In fact, great customer service lies at the root of companies that are disrupting the way certain industries have always operated.

Look no further than Amazon and Uber to see this in practice. Amazon has turned retail on its head by providing convenience and great service. Because of this, both brick-and-mortar storefronts and competing online retailers are closing left and right. Meanwhile, Uber offered an alternative to the horrible customer service that cab companies were almost universally known for, transforming the transportation industry in the process. Both of these examples show us that customer service is shaping how companies move forward and that customers will follow.

Loyalty is generated when a customer consistently enjoys

a great customer experience at your business. After a while, they stop even considering your competitors.

Critical to any outstanding customer experience is making your customer feel valued. They want to feel like they are appreciated by the providers and faces of the brand, product, or service they're paying for. As we'll discuss in the pages to come, there are several ways of accomplishing this. However, one of the biggest is simply saying, "Thank you. Thank you for coming in today."

Giving customers this experience of feeling appreciated begins by making employees feel like they're appreciated.

THE EMPLOYEE EXPERIENCE

Particularly in retail, hospitality, and restaurant environments, much of the frontline staff generally consists of entry-level positions.The employees filling these roles generally aren't being paid a lot. This dynamic can lead to high turnover.

Turnover is problematic because maintaining a certain level of service requires consistency. Consistency and a revolving workforce door don't go hand in hand. Often, budgets don't allow for this turnover to be resolved by throwing money at it and raising wages.

Having been an entry-level service employee myself at the beginning of my career, it was obvious to me from day one as a manager that creating a great working environment for my employees was nothing short of essential. If you want your employees to be loyal to you, there has to be some motivation.

Here's the great news: creating that motivation is completely under your control, and it requires no additional expense aside from your genuine care and concern for their well-being and day-to-day experience. While you may very well not have any control over your company's budget, what you *do* have control over is the opportunity to create a positive impact on your employees.

This also creates an exciting opportunity for you. In many cases, you will be the first leader your team members ever experience. Even if you're not, you can still serve as an example of what a great manager looks like. You will model to your staff what it means to be a leader. You have a rare opportunity, which is to set an example that will set the standard for someone from this day forward.

To this day, I still emulate Brian Perkins, the general manager from my first job, where I worked the front desk at a hotel. Despite the fact that I had no previous hotel experience, he saw something in me, gave me a shot, and cultivated my strengths. In very real ways, I am where I am today because of him.

You have the power and the privilege to do that for someone too.

YOUR TOP PRIORITY AS A LEADER

You can start bettering your workplace culture today by doing this one simple thing: make time for your team members every single day. Make time to say hello, to say thank you, to acknowledge something that they've done, big or small.

I consider this interaction to be so important that I make an intentional effort of building it into my everyday routine. In fact, getting face time with my employees is the first thing I do every day. Don't get me wrong—this isn't always easy. There have been plenty of times when I've arrived at work with my cell phone buzzing away in my pocket and important emails and voice mails that I know need my attention. Here's the thing, though: this is life. Those other priorities are never going to stop. So you have to make a decision that connecting and building a relationship with your employees is also a priority. In fact, nine times out of ten, it should be *the* priority.

This all begins with "Thanks for coming in today," but

it goes beyond that too. You want to connect with your staff on a personal level and allow them to see that you genuinely care about them—not just as employees but as people.

For me, that meant not even stepping into my office until I'd already been at work for a couple of hours. Those first two hours of every day were spent hitting the marble, as we call it in the hotel industry. In that time, I made sure that I visited every single department.

These walkabouts gave me the opportunity to build awareness about what was going on with employees not only on a professional basis but also on a personal one. I would talk to team members as I would speak to my friends.

I made a point of asking how their move went, how their baby was doing, if they were excited about their upcoming vacation. Remembering this volume of personal information isn't always easy. However, it's incredibly important and worth putting some practice into. If something seemed particularly critical—for example, if an employee's mother was ill—or if I was feeling especially frazzled, sometimes I would even make a note to myself to be sure to follow up on that situation the next time I saw an employee. Yes, this might seem impersonal, but when you are managing a large volume of staff, it's also realistic.

As I got to know my employees better over time, I was able to gauge where they were. For example, I might notice that a usually chatty employee was quieter than usual or that someone who was always calm appeared to be stressed out. It gave me the opportunity to understand how they were doing and to see if they needed to talk or needed help, even if they didn't explicitly vocalize it.

Aside from everything else, this type of management style also breeds accountability. Your staff knows that you are acutely aware of what they are and are not doing. Employees are less likely to call out or to be unproductive because they understand what they do matters and is seen. They are invested in their job.

By the time two hours had passed, I had made some sort of personal contact with every single employee under my charge. It set the tone for the day—not only for me but for employees as well. It provided us with structure and instilled confidence in employees that I was always aware of what was going on. It created a culture of self-worth and of trust. My team members wanted to give 100 percent because they knew that I was giving them 100 percent and that I cared about their well-being.

THE TRICKLE-DOWN EFFECT OF ENGAGEMENT

While I don't believe that thanking and interacting with

employees was the reason our Marriott soared in rankings, I do believe it laid the foundation for creating the positive environment we needed to get us to that point. It's as simple as this: employees who feel valued make customers feel valued.

As with employees, the beginning of instilling a sense of appreciation in customers begins with small but important measures. What's the easiest and most fundamental way of establishing this? Well, of course, by thanking customers for coming in today. After all, even more so than employees, you customers don't *have* to come in. There are plenty of other options for them to choose from. This gratitude should be genuine because, at the end of the day, the combined impact of these singular customer decisions is literally responsible for the fact that you have a job.

Regardless of your employee culture, expressing gratitude to customers on a regular and consistent basis should be part of your customer service culture. However, when employees are conditioned with this practice and experience the impact of it on their own psyche, it becomes almost innate and so much more heartfelt. Customers can feel this, even if they can't put their finger on what it is that feels so different about your establishment.

IN SUMMARY

Sometimes it feels like some of these more intangible elements of building culture might not really be worth it. Taking a couple of hours out of your day—or any amount of time, for that matter—to do something that often feels like chatting is a big ask of any leader in the service industry. Not only that, but the results aren't always easy to measure.

I promise you that it's worth it. When I took over that Marriott in Cincinnati, semiannual employee surveys ranked us as one of the least engaged hotels in our company. In the two years I was there, we moved that engagement score up by a full ten points and were ranked as one of the most engaged properties in the company. During that same period of time, we were voted one of Cincinnati's Best Places to Work. Not only that, but we were the only hotel on the list. It's no coincidence that our customer service rankings shot through the roof in this same time period.

These things do matter and they do affect change, even if it doesn't always feel like that on a day-to-day basis. Bill Marriott had it right when he said, "If you take care of your employees, they'll take care of the customer." If customer service is your goal, it all begins with how you treat your employees—not when you need something but on a regular and consistent basis.

CHAPTER TWO

First Impressions Matter

———

Your team members' experience of working for your company begins from the very first point of contact they have as an applicant. Immediately, their opinions are being formed about what it means to work for you. This is why onboarding is so important. In fact, a recent article in *HR Daily Advisor* points to the fact that 91 percent of employees remain with a company for at least a year, and 69 percent remain for at least three years if a company has a well-structured onboarding program. Talk about a huge payoff!

THE HIRING PROCESS

Very few companies put the attention they should into the experience of applying for a position. Everyone should, for two very important reasons. The first is that from the moment a candidate logs on to your website or picks up an application, they are absorbing cues about your company and what service means to you.

Secondly, applicants are also either customers or potential customers. Even if they don't ultimately get the job, your business may very well have an ongoing relationship with them in some capacity. Just like any other customer or employee relationship, you want to nurture your relationship with applicants.

FINDING THE RIGHT PEOPLE

In a perfect world, your dream candidate would just show up on your doorstep. Unfortunately, finding a great customer-experience-oriented employee can require some sorting. Let's look at some key points of the hiring process that will help you find just the person you're looking for.

Often, the process of curating candidate options is done at the discretion of the human resources department, but I've found it's helpful to give HR an idea of what I'm looking for. I have come to believe that most people like serving others for the simple reason that it feels good to make other people happy. However, certain people have developed more of a skillset around service than others.

Some people are great at coding, others are great at painting a picture, and some are born to serve. Those are the people you want to identify and bring onboard.

If you notice some common key attributes among your preexisting star employees, be sure to let HR (or whoever comes into first contact with potential employees) know what those are so that they can screen for them both in the job posting and during initial conversations with candidates.

Over the years, I have learned that candidates with a positive attitude, high energy level, and sense of presence do very well in customer service. I also look out for people who have a history of volunteer work, are involved in their community, and are excited to talk about their family. All of this provides promising clues about how you can expect that person to interact with others.

STAY ON THE LOOKOUT

As a leader in the service industry, you already know that one of the biggest issues confronting all of us is finding the right people. For this reason, a sense of urgency is always required. If someone great finds their way to you, it's critical that they put in an application and you hire them right then and there, on the spot. Time and time again, I lost someone great because I didn't act immediately. Great candidates are going to find a job, and they're going to find it quickly. Time is of the essence.

It is a best—if not essential—practice to make sure that any employees stationed at the front of house (receptionists, hostesses, front desk agents, etc.) are trained to identify the qualities you are looking for in an ideal job applicant. This is how you will ensure that great candidates don't slip through your fingers. As an added bonus, it will instill an additional sense of ownership in that team member.

If a potential candidate who looks the part walks through your business doors, don't let them leave. That's how I got hired. I saw an ad in the newspaper, put on a shirt and tie, drove to the hotel, and walked out with a job three hours later.

No matter what else may be going on at the moment an applicant arrives, make speaking with them a priority. This small sacrifice of your time could be a great investment for your business. If need be, ask them to wait and offer them a drink or appetizer (or whatever else is available) in the interim. Treat them like a customer. Demonstrate to them what hospitality means in your business.

JOB POSTING

I've noticed that there often seems to be a disconnect between the person writing a job description and general brand messaging. Remember that not everyone who sees your job posting will apply. Some of the readers will be (or already are) customers. Job postings should be an extension of who and what your brand is. After all, you want to find employees who align with your brand philosophy and what it stands for.

While you may very well not be the person writing the job posting, you will generally have the chance to give it a once-over. Aside from checking for consistent messaging, also notice if the job description needs to be spiced up. Remember that your potential candidates are looking at other job postings as well. You want yours to stand out so that you can attract the highest-caliber employees. By all means, do not stretch the truth and make the job or your company sound like something they're not. That's a tactic that will only backfire in the long run. *Do* remember, though, that good people want to work good jobs for good companies. Make sure your job and your company sound like a situation that outstanding employees will want to be a part of.

All of this might sound a little bit overboard. Trust me, it's not. Today, the biggest challenge companies face is finding and retaining great talent. That's right. It's not creating more product or finding more customers; it's finding great people to be on your team. According to a 2017 report from the National Restaurant Association, 37 percent of its members said labor recruitment was their top challenge, up from just 15 percent two years earlier. Just like you are selling customers on the fact that your company is the best, you're also selling employees. A little extra effort is well worth your time and energy in the long run.

You won't always have control over all of the communication that goes on between your company and a candidate, especially during the early parts of the hiring process. But remember, every bit of communication from the first touch point on conveys a message about how your company treats others and the kind of service it provides.

When it's appropriate, I might approach the person who is either overseeing or having those initial conversations with candidates and say something along the lines of "Hey, can you please walk me through the applicant process?" If I find out the person leading up the charge is someone I haven't worked with before, I might offer a very gentle—and extremely respectful—reminder that they will be providing the applicant with the first glimpse of our company's service.

Likewise, you want whoever has first contact with potential employees to be screening them immediately as well. How do they interact on the phone? What about emails? All of these are important clues that give you an idea of the type of customer service you can expect from a potential employee.

I feel it's important that the highest-ranking person in any customer service organization personally meets with candidates before they are hired as part of the final interview. This is an integral part of building your customer service experience to the greatest degree—ensuring that every person on your team is a good fit and of the right mindset for the service environment you are creating.

Since employees have already been prescreened before I interview them, our meeting generally consists of two primary questions that tend to let me know everything I need to know. For example, if I managed a spa, the first question I would ask is "What do you look for when you walk into a spa?" This same question can be applied to any industry. While this is somewhat of a softball question since most candidates will reply that they want it to be clean or expect good service, you're beginning to instill a very important mindset—that you want your employees to put themselves in the customers' shoes.

The second question—which I consider to be crucial— is "If you could do any job in the world, why would you choose to serve people?" The answer that I love most to hear is something along the lines of "Because it makes my day to see someone smile," "I like to make people feel good," or "I want to impact someone else's day in a positive way." This is a good clue that the person sitting across from me is wired to thrive in the type of environment I want to create. When I hear people give this type of answer, I know they were born with a service hospitality mindset and will thrive in this position.

A few times, an otherwise perfectly qualified and experienced candidate has gotten to the point of speaking with me and provided an answer that's more along the lines of "I'm looking for a part-time job" or any other number of responses that have nothing to do with service or interaction. No matter how much I need to fill the position or what kind of previous job experience they bring to the table, I always pass. This type of response is a clear red flag that they're not going to have the skin in the game my team needs in order to meet the level of service we want to provide.

There are a few other cues I look for in a potential employee that give me a good idea of how they'll interact with guests. When they're waiting for our interview in the lobby, I notice their body language. Are they smiling at people as they walk by? As we speak, I take note of whether or not they are engaging in our conversation. Are they polite? Do they make eye contact? Do I sense genuine excitement? All of these things are important and will translate well with customers.

It's easy to get caught up in hiring based on experience

and background. The truth is you can teach anyone the rote tasks they need to perform. You *can't* teach an attitude or instill in someone the desire to want to help others. It's these intangible qualities that matter most. Over the years, I've hired plenty of people with literally no work experience. What they *do* have is a great attitude and a genuine excitement about serving people. Not once have I regretted one of those hires.

Many years ago, I interviewed a woman for a front-desk position whose personality was downright infectious. She had no experience whatsoever in the hotel business. I passed her right through, but she failed a mandatory personality assessment that the hotel required all potential employees to take. It was company policy that you had to pass this test in order to work for the hotel. Still, this woman had crushed our interview, and I knew in my gut she would be incredible in the position. I had to have her on my team.

I bent the rules and had her retake the test after some coaching. This was a big no-no, but I didn't care. I needed to get her where she had to be so that I could hire her. Fifteen years later, she is now a highly successful hotel industry sales manager.

The most important action I took in that situation was to listen to my gut. If your gut tells you someone isn't right for your team despite the fact that you can't pinpoint why that might be, they're not your person. End of story.

One final caution when it comes to hiring: in the service industry, it can be easy to settle for someone who is "good enough" because your team is overtaxed and you need to fill a position. In the moment, it might seem like any warm body will do. I can tell you that every single time I've fallen into that trap, it has backfired.

After years of experience, I have learned the hard way that I would much rather suffer through leaving a position open for as long as it takes than putting the wrong person in a role. Logistically, it is difficult to exit people. It is also difficult to coach someone who is not the right fit. You end up spinning your wheels and, in the end, spend a lot more time, energy, and money working with someone who has been cast in the wrong position than you would have if you had just waited it out to hire the right person.

CREATE A WELCOMING ENVIRONMENT

When it comes to onboarding, I think Dustin DiChiara, who owns a Chick-fil-A, has got it right. In the 2018 American Consumer Satisfaction Index, Chick-fil-A received a rating of 87 out of 100 for the third year in a row in the limited service category. Its closest competitor, Panera, was a distant second, with a rating of 81. Clearly, Chick-fil-A is a leader in customer satisfaction.

DiChiara has every new employee spend their first day at the restaurant's administrative office rather than the storefront, where it is much more distracting and difficult to focus. While it may not always be possible to utilize multiple locations, it is possible to incorporate the sort of intentional process DiChiara exemplifies in terms of making time for new employees throughout the onboarding process.

Even if you are onboarding a team member at the same location where business occurs, you can make sure the two of you are away from the front lines, where it's less chaotic. You want to get yourself into a situation that allows you to give your full attention to the new hire. This is especially important because I've noticed this special sort of Murphy's Law: Onboarding days always tend to be the craziest days. This makes it easy to lose focus on the important task at hand in favor of putting out fires and dealing with day-to-day business. Also, if it does get crazy, it can be intimidating to employees. You want to ease them into the fray and allow them to connect with you before hitting the front lines.

Making this sort of space for employees—even for a relatively small portion of time—communicates a lot. It sets the tone for the sort of experience an employee can expect working with you. You are also serving as the representative of your brand. On a subconscious level, you're emulating the sort of attention and experience that your brand wants to create and that you expect the employee to create for customers.

I'm sure that you've had plenty of first days at work, so you can relate to the fact that starting a new job can be nerve-racking. It's even more so when you feel like you're in the way or don't belong. If an employee starts off feeling cast away, it can be a difficult feeling to reverse. Having an organized process helps by greatly reducing the chances a new hire will feel as though they are lost in the shuffle or floating out there on their own.

You can minimize an employee's first-day nerves by creating a structured approach. Before they even arrive, let them know what to expect—when and where you'll be meeting, where to park, what to wear, who to ask for, and any other details they'll need to make their arrival as smooth as possible. This might sound like minutiae, but have you ever been in a panic when you've arrived at an important meeting only to find a confusing parking situation? It can be enough to throw your entire day off, particularly if you end up running late or are harried because of it.

Another big part of making each employee feel welcome,

important, and acknowledged is having everything they'll need ready to roll by the time they arrive. This includes tiny details like having their email account (if they have one) set up and ready to log in to, name tags printed and waiting for them, and a folder with their paperwork all set. Just like details matter to customers (which we'll discuss in depth in Chapter 7), they also matter to team members.

Finally, make sure that either you or a direct manager are there to greet the new hire on their first day. I'm always shocked when a department manager schedules a new person on their day off. This leaves so much room for error, and there's no amount of planning that will keep the new hire from falling through the cracks to some degree. No one else will care about the newest member of your department as much as you do.

The person meeting the new hire should have a firm understanding of the importance of onboarding, how it's structured, and your expectations. Furthermore, I always like to assign a buddy to the new person. The buddy system doesn't have to involve anything more than ensuring the new hire has someone to eat lunch with that first day, but it still allows them to begin to build their network and start feeling like part of the team. It can be difficult to be an outsider, at a loss for where to even begin making connections. Again, put yourself in their position—being a new hire can feel a lot like the first day of school all over again. It's intimidating. Do everything in your power to make it less so.

Your onboarding experience is one of the first glimpses team members will have of what it's like to work at your company. It's also their first look at what service means for your brand. Just like they will be serving the customer, you are serving the employee. Things that might seem small or even inconsequential—like being disheveled or disorganized—matter. They convey very real cues that can potentially set a tone you don't want to communicate.

Most importantly, you're showing new employees they matter. Right off the bat, you're telling them their presence is appreciated and important. They are a priority and the most important item on your agenda during that time you are spending together. Much like you create an experience for customers, you also create an ongoing experience for employees. Onboarding is a particularly critical touch point within that experience.

IN SUMMARY

It sounds almost too simple, but the bottom line is that you can't offer a great customer experience without great employees on hand to provide it. Of course, you want employees who execute and are responsible. However, even the most technically proficient and efficient employee won't add what your team needs if they are not service-oriented.

By keeping this at the top of your mind throughout the interview and onboarding process, you will find the people you need to create a stellar customer service environment, and you will make them feel invested in your team from day one. Employees who feel appreciated create customers who feel appreciated.

CHAPTER THREE

Set the Bar

———

On my first day in the hotel business, Brian, the general manager, handed me a list of expectations. At first, it struck me as odd, but as he walked me through the twenty or so items on the list, I understood why this document was so important: It provided a framework for how he was going to operate and what he expected of me. Basically, he showed me how to succeed. There was no mystery to it, as it was all outlined on this piece of paper. I appreciated the gesture because it allowed me to act with more immediate confidence and to get started on the right foot in an environment I wasn't yet acquainted with.

This experience stuck with me. As I moved forward in my career, I always maintained an expectation document. This document evolved as I evolved as a leader.

Whenever I started managing a new hotel, I shared this

document with other department managers within the first week. Their initial reaction was always the same: Who is this new guy, and what the heck is this document? By the time we reached the end of the second page, I could feel the room shift. Sharing expectations ultimately puts everyone at ease. It lets them understand not only what is expected of them but also what they can expect of you as a leader. There is a lot of comfort in that.

SAMPLE EXPECTATIONS

Your expectations should be personal, although there are certain elements that will probably appear on every service industry leader's list of must-dos. Following is my list of expectations, which you can use to brainstorm and get you started. You will notice that these expectations include not only what I expect from my team members but also what they can expect from me.

Dear Team,

Following is a list of the basic expectations I have of us as a leadership team. It will provide the framework for how we operate.

1. Guest satisfaction is our number one priority. It is every team member's responsibility to ensure world-class guest satisfaction through passionate service delivery and by a whatever-it-takes attitude.
2. Our employees are the foundation of our success or failure. Create an environment where both you and your team genuinely want to come to work every day. Never pass an employee without greeting them. Treat each employee just as you would a customer.
3. We will be problem solvers, not problem identifiers. When you see a problem, be ready to discuss a solution for fixing it.
4. Attitude is everything. As leaders, we don't get the luxury of having a bad or off day in front of our guests, counterparts, or team members. We will have a positive attitude at all times, in all circumstances. If you need to vent, I am here for you, but it must be behind closed doors. Whatever fire you are putting out or issue you are facing, you will get through it.
5. Empower your associates to solve guest issues and excel at service recovery. Replace the phrase "I have to check with the manager" with "I can help you."
6. Work schedules are always dependent on business levels. Your department is your responsibility. On your days off, you must ensure your department is adequately covered.
7. Remember, you are a manager, and as such, you represent the entire brand. Take that responsibility seriously.
8. We will be consistent. Our operation should run the same way day in and day out.

9. If you need me, don't hesitate to call. I will always make myself available to you.

10. If a guest asks whether you are a manager, the appropriate answer is "Yes, I am one of the managers. How may I help you?" Own their request or issue through completion.

11. The property will be immaculate. This includes back-of-the-house areas and meeting rooms, which should be treated with the same attention to detail as guest areas.

12. Your quality of life is important to me. Come to work, contribute to the team, then go home and enjoy your time off.

13. We are a team. Always be available to help other departments.

14. Any meeting, whether with staff or clients, is important. Come prepared and be on time ("on time" means early). Show respect to the individual who is speaking—no side conversations.

15. I encourage any and all feedback. Don't hesitate to ask questions or suggest ways for us to improve.

16. Don't be afraid to make a decision. If it ends up being a mistake, that's okay. Learn from it and move on. Your fellow teammates and I are here to support you.

17. We will exceed expectations in every respect, including standards, cleanliness, service, and financials.

18. I am a big believer in professionalism. Always be aware of what you are saying and who you are saying it to. You never know who is listening. There is no room for profanity in the workplace. We have a responsibility to create an environment where our team members look forward to coming in to work each day.

19. Don't let customers see the business side of our business.

20. Inspect what you expect.

WHY EXPECTATIONS MATTER

It's easy to assume your team automatically understands what you expect of them. However, that's not always the case. This is particularly true in industries where there is a lot of turnover. People come and go, team members are trained by different higher-ups, and the same information isn't always conveyed. Official expectations ensure everyone is working with the same information, playing on the same team, and following the same rules.

This works in big and small ways. Let's say, for example, someone cusses in the kitchen. You, as the leader, have taken for granted that everyone knows this is not the tone you want to set at your establishment. However, this employee has worked in that same kitchen for six years and never once has he been told not to cuss. Now, in the heat of the moment, you have to lay down the law. Likely, it won't be effective. In fact, it will probably only add to everyone's frustration. It's also not entirely fair to the employee. Expectations mitigate situations like this through prevention as opposed to reaction.

ESTABLISHING YOUR EXPECTATIONS

Your expectations should touch on elements like guest satisfaction, employee satisfaction, cleanliness standards, brand standards, and leadership.

I also like to provide each team member with a set of service basics (which are very much also an expectation) in the form of a card they can keep with them. Many establishments have some form of service expectations, and they generally contain much of the same content.

I'm shocked when a company doesn't have service basics

in place. It is these basics that set the groundwork for a good customer experience. For example, Ritz-Carlton has a Credo Card that is part of the employee uniform. Each team member carries one on them at all times. This card lists the company's service beliefs. Credo Cards are so legendary that staff members sometimes give theirs away to guests as a keepsake. You can view the Credo online under the Gold Standards section at RitzCarlton. com.

There's nothing complex on this Credo Card. It simply serves as a reminder of what's most important. It ensures that everyone is on the same page and understands what good service looks like in their culture.

Before every shift, Ritz-Carlton has a ritual called Line Up. At Line Up, the manager chooses a service point and explains how it was put into action the day before. This is used as a way of framing the company's service beliefs in real-world situations. Many companies have similar traditions to set the tone for the day. It's a way of engraining service basics and also of recognizing employees for good work.

There is one thing to note here. While I am a huge proponent of service basics, you also have to be careful not to box staff members in. For example, if someone asks for directions to the restroom, and your company policy is not to point but to guide, it doesn't necessarily mean your staff members need to lead guests into the bathroom. Some employees take service basics so literally that they follow them through to the letter, even in situations that might not be appropriate. It's important to leave room for employees to read the customer and determine what they need on a case-by-case basis. For example, a chattier guest may want to engage with an employee and chat all the way to the restroom, while a more introverted guest is happier not to.

It's also important that your staff members understand the spirit behind the law. For example, some companies mandate team members respond to a customer "Thank you" with the reply "My pleasure." The issue here is that some people find "My pleasure" to be a scripted response. The truth is it *can* sound scripted if employees don't understand *why* they are saying it. When phrases like this come from an authentic place, they read as genuine rather than rote.

Also, understand that setting expectations is not enough. As a leader, you also have to live them out. No card or expectation letter will take the place of action, no matter how thorough or well written they are. For example, if you tell your staff members to escort customers to their desired destination, but you don't do it yourself, you can be sure your employees never will either.

To get you started, I have included some service expectations that have served me well over the years. Feel free to use these to get you started. Add on and omit information as you see fit and as works best for your business and your goals.

SERVICE BASICS

- Be hospitable.
- Practice the 15/5 Rule by making eye contact and smiling whenever you are within fifteen feet any customer and offer a verbal exchange within five feet (such as "Good morning" or "How are you?").
- Show sincere empathy when a customer has a complaint, then make it right. You are empowered.
- Whenever possible, use the customer's name.
- Replace "You're welcome" with "My pleasure."
- Replace "No problem" with "It would be my pleasure" or "Certainly."
- Always own a customer request and personally ensure it is completed.
- Escort rather than point when asked for directions.
- Never say no. Instead focus on and say what you can do.
- Answer the phone with a positive tone of voice within three rings.
- Take pride in the cleanliness and maintenance of your property, including always reporting safety concerns or items in need of repair.
- Take pride in how you look, and always look your best.
- Be a team player—actively look for opportunities to assist your teammates.

EXPECTATIONS THAT WORK

Every company's expectations will look slightly different, but over the years, I have found a few of them to be particularly critical. You will note that many of the expectations listed in the expectations document sample at the beginning of this chapter appear throughout the pages of this book, at least in sentiment. However, there are a few more specific expectations that I would recommend considering as you begin to think through establishing your own.

NO BAD DAYS

When you are elevated into a leadership position, you shed some rights. One of the biggest is the luxury of having an off or bad day. Like it or not, as a leader, you set the tone for the day. At some point, every one of us has worked for a manager who makes no bones about the type of mood they're in on any given day. There's nothing worse than being in a position in which you have to tiptoe around, wondering what sort of mood your boss is in.

We all have bad days, but the minute you walk in the door at work, you're on. Let your managers know that you do acknowledge they are human and will have bad days. However, the appropriate response isn't to put this on display for their team members. Instead, anyone in a leadership role should come talk to you in your office or outside of the building. It can't happen in front of the staff. Of course, all of this applies to you as well. A manager's bad mood impacts team members' ability to give

100 percent of their attention and energy to customer service. They're too busy worrying about their manager.

You will have trying days in the service industry. Everyone does. We are dealing with people, and sometimes that gets messy or chaotic. Keep things in perspective. The sky is not always falling. This day will pass, and whatever you're dealing with in the moment won't matter in the long run. Things always works themselves out. The calmer you remain, the easier it will be to deal with the issue at hand.

Remember that your staff can be intimidated by management. Your title comes with stereotypes and implications. Whether you like it or not, when you're a leader, you are being watched, and people are feeding off your energy.

When I was an assistant general manager, hotel management would revert to me for the night when the general manager left at 5:00. One evening, the GM decided he wanted to stay later than usual to observe how things were operating. That night happened to be a bit more chaotic than usual, particularly in the restaurant. While it's true that it was hectic, our staff was a well-oiled machine and had everything under control. Still, the GM was barking out orders and getting red in the face because tables weren't getting food as fast as he wanted them to.

As I watched on, I realized the GM was making the situation worse, not better. I knew the employees, and I understood their strengths. We had experienced nights like this before, and we always came through successfully. That night, they were scared and on edge, which caused them to make mistakes they normally wouldn't. The GM wasn't a bad guy, but on this particular night, his presence and demeanor impacted the environment in a negative way. As a leader, this is something it's imperative to always be aware of. Staff feeds off your mood and demeanor.

As for your employees, they will have bad days too. They are also human. As a manager, there are some days when you might feel like a therapist. If someone's pet dies before they come in or their relationship has broken up, their work is likely going to reflect that. You can view this as an opportunity to show your leadership and concern for your team members in a holistic sense. You might offer them the opportunity to go home for the day or even to provide a listening ear. If they opt to stay at work, you might move them behind the scenes so that they can work without impacting the customer.

WORK ISN'T YOUR WHOLE LIFE

It wasn't until later on in my career that I realized work was a *part* of my life rather than my actual life. I've seen a similar thing happen to a lot of people in the service industry, especially salaried employees. In this game, it's entirely possible to work a ridiculous number of hours. Whereas, in some industries, business closes at 5:00 and you're done, that is not the case for us. Your business might be open 365 days a year until all hours. If you are wired to stay at your job while everyone else is there, you're eventually going to burn out. The reality is that you can't be there all of the time. More than that, you *shouldn't* be there all of the time.

When a manager's time is up for the day, I expect and want them to go home. They will be more effective at their job if they take time away to decompress and rejuvenate. Work should be enjoyable, but it's not going to be if you never leave. And if you don't enjoy work, you won't do a good job. No one should judge anyone else for going home when it's time. Work is a part of life, not your entire life.

I learned this lesson the hard way. I was in a relationship that wasn't working because I worked all of the time. For a few years, I left the hotel industry to work in private aviation so that I could have some time back. In the end, I returned to the hotel industry because I missed it. I was born with hospitality in my blood and felt myself being called back to a life that allowed me to be a part of a team and impact customers.

When I came back, I was a little bit older and more

mature. I understood that I had to maintain a quality of life outside of work. I had to find balance between doing a good job and still making outside work and life a priority. Since I wanted that balance, I wanted everyone around me to have it as well. I am now proactive about making sure employees leave when they need to.

PROVIDE FEEDBACK

Ruling with an iron fist rarely works in this day and age. As frontline representatives, your employees are a wonderful resource. They have the inside loop on what can make the business run more smoothly. This is the entire value of having a team. If you're reading this book, you probably already realize this.

Employee feedback should also include how *you* can do better. There may be instances when feedback can't or shouldn't be incorporated, but you still always want to have an open mind and an open door to it.

Sometimes feedback about how you are managing can feel personal. This is particularly true if you work for a company that conducts anonymous surveys. Unfiltered feedback can be brutal. The reality is that even if you are the greatest leader and nicest person around, there are still going to be people who don't like you. You can't be everything to everyone, so as a leader, you have to develop a layer of thick skin for those moments when this occurs. Even if it hurts, and even if it's not always accurate, feedback is still important.

As a leader, it's up to you to maturely differentiate between what can and should be changed, and what is simply irrelevant, personal opinion.

DON'T SHOW THE BUSINESS BEHIND YOUR BUSINESS

Recently, I walked through a restaurant and noticed that the door to the manager's office was open. I could clearly see the manager sitting at a table working on her computer. Another time when I was at my local grocery store, the employee monitoring self-checkout was sitting around munching on a Lunchable, talking about another employee who wasn't working hard enough and needed to be fired.

When you are at work, you are onstage. Your customers are watching you, whether you realize it or not. As with any other production, you don't want your audience to see behind the curtain. It takes away the mystique and magic. When we are going into a business as a customer, we go not to think but to have an experience. Being reminded that you are at a business and seeing how that business operates behind the scenes can detract from the experience.

Don't let people see into your office. Don't have work conversations in any situation where a customer might potentially hear. Don't let customers be privy to any of the behind-the-scenes action that might take away from the magic.

INSPECT WHAT YOU EXPECT

Beyond setting expectations, it's also your job as a leader to make sure those expectations are met. I refer to this as "inspecting what you expect." It simply refers to the fact that it's up to you and your management team to make sure that your company is living up to your standards—and moreover, that each and every team member plays the role required of them to accomplish this.

You can tell a team member you want one hundred rolls of silverware ready to go at 9:00 a.m. However, if they know you are never going to hold them accountable, some motivation might be lacking. I'm not suggesting you micromanage and hover over team members' shoulders, but I am advising that you manage by walking around (more on this in Chapter 5) and remain on top of everything happening within your company. This will provide a clear—although perhaps subconscious—cue that everyone is held accountable for following through on what's expected of them, as your team will understand you are out and about, observing what's happening at all times.

When I do have to nudge team members to follow through with expectations, I always do so in the form of asking rather than telling. I'll say something like "Hey, can you do me a favor and make sure those one hundred napkin rolls are taken care of?" This might sound like a small detail, but it has a big impact over time. If you ask someone to do you a favor—even if that favor is an integral part of their job—they are more inclined to do so and to do so happily.

MOTIVATING TEAM MEMBERS

There are any number of ways to motivate team members to hit and exceed expectations, and one of my favorite ways is to incorporate some fun into the process. It's a great morale booster and often requires little to no expenditure.

One of my favorite examples of mixing fun and motivation involves a dirty retention pond. I know—doesn't sound very fun or motivating, right? But it was. I set the lofty goal for my team to achieve the number one ranking for customer service within our company. To have some fun with this, I promised the staff that when we hit this goal, I would jump into the retention pond behind our hotel.

The mental image of me jumping into the pond became

a joke that we could all rally around, especially during meetings and pep rallies (more on this in Chapter 5). It was a playful topic that we could reference and that I, specifically, could use in place of more "managerial" asks or prompts. For instance, instead of reminding a team member to greet every customer they came into contact with, I could instead say something like "Hey, don't you want to see me go for a swim in the pond?" This would achieve the same purpose but allow for a much different tone in our manager-employee relationship.

IN SUMMARY

It's important to set your team up for success. Achieving goals as part of a team and hitting personal milestones instill a sense of pride, both collectively and individually. This pride translates into more ownership and a greater sense of investment in the company as a whole, as well as the team member's day-to-day role within it—very much including customer service.

CHAPTER FOUR

Lead, Don't Manage

———

One of the most important tools I have in my management arsenal is my running shoes.

In the hotel industry—as with the service industry in general—it's difficult to meet "rush" staffing needs. You don't always know when rushes are going to hit. Not only that, but these busy periods often happen in short bursts. It doesn't make financial sense to have a ton of people on the clock to handle a thirty-minute window of time. In those moments when three buses show up simultaneously or half of the hotel decides to eat breakfast at the same time, leaders have to jump into the fray—or at least they should.

I once worked at a downtown hotel where many conferences were held. There were bursts of time when everyone would arrive for or leave an event all at once, and the valet stand would go crazy. Of course, it didn't make sense for us to bring in eight extra valets to handle that single hour. Aside from being a budgetary issue, bringing on all of those additional people would also mean that the valets' tips were significantly diluted. As a result, the staff we did have on hand was stretched to their limit during intense moments.

It didn't take me long to learn to keep an extra pair of running shoes in my office so that when those moments hit, I could serve as another hand on deck. Before long, other managers noticed I was running around pulling cars in and out of the lot, so they started chipping in at the valet stand too. The best part is that I never asked them to. You'll quickly find that when you're willing to pitch in, other people are too. It's contagious.

After a while, the valets knew that when they were maxed out, they could throw out a Bat Signal, and we managers would come sprinting. They also knew we would put any tips we received back into their pockets so they weren't losing out on income that was important to them by calling upon us.

The same principle applies to the front desk, the restaurant, and any other department you can think of—although those departments might not require running shoes.

Pitching in is no skin off my back. In fact, I often find it to be a good break in my day, and it's the perfect opportunity to get on the ground and mingle with employees and guests to see how things are running (no pun intended). It also earns me a lot of trust and respect from my employees because they realize that not only am I more than willing to help, but I will also do anything I ask of them myself. It removes some of the invisible barriers between us.

I once worked at a company where everyone joked that the only time a certain manager would make an appearance on the lower level—where the lobby and employee areas were located—was when she had to use the restroom. While this was told as a joke, it's indicative of a bigger problem: How can employees be invested in a team whose captain is an elusive, faceless figure?

To be truly excited about what they're doing and who they're doing it for, employees have to feel like their leaders have some skin in the game too. They have to know you're going to back them up, especially when the going gets tough. Few things are as motivating as a manager who demonstrates that they're invested in the team—and more than that, a manager who shows they consider themselves to be a *part* of the same team as their employees.

WE, NOT ME

Small actions build a "we" versus "me" philosophy. For as long as I've been working, it's always rubbed me the wrong way when it feels like leadership is on one level and the rest of the staff is on another, lower level. This can be communicated in big and small ways. For example, it's communicated when a manager isn't willing to do the same things they ask of staff. It's also implicit in seemingly innocuous statements like "*My* team did X."

I don't want to own a team. I want to be *part of* a team. A team that's ours, not mine. I want a team that sees how invested I am in the work at hand so that they will be too. Not only do I want to consider myself part of a team, but I also want my cohorts to. I've noticed that when I refer to "we" and "our," after a while, employees begin doing the same. I don't know about you, but I would much rather be working with a team than be working at a job.

BE PRESENT

Being part of a team means being present. I have worked for managers and other leaders who spent their entire day behind a desk. You can't be an integral part of a team if no one ever sees you. When this is the case, there are actually two teams, albeit teams that are playing in tandem—us and them.

When you hide out behind a desk—particularly during the crazy periods of the day—you are missing out on an opportunity. You can elevate an entire team by making them genuinely want to do better and pitch in when you exemplify that same willingness.

The truth is you may not know everything about every single job and department under your supervision, and that's okay. Great leaders understand they don't need to know everything; however, you do need to understand a little about everything. You learn this by getting out in the trenches. No one expects you to be the best at every role you are filling or task you are performing at any given moment in time. The important thing is that you are present.

The best leaders I've run across embrace what they don't know. They trust their team members to perform the roles they are hired for, and they understand the leadership role is often most effective when it's a background role that involves supporting the team in whatever way necessary.

For example, I know how to cook, but I am not by any means a chef. There is no doubt in my mind that the executive chef I manage knows far more than I do. (We'd all be in big trouble if he didn't!) So when the restaurant gets slammed, I'm certainly not going to jump on the line and try to make some steaks—but I'm also not going to hide out in my office. Instead, I'm going to work on the other side of the line putting plates together. I'm going to fit in where I can to alleviate some of the pressure so that the other team members can do what they do best.

This same concept applies to pretty much any department or function in the service industry. When your team needs help, there's always somewhere you can fit in. Often, it's going to be in those unglamorous, behind-the-scenes jobs. Roll up your sleeves (or strap on your shoes) and get in there! As an added bonus, your staff will get a kick out of seeing you tie on an apron and do some dishes. It can be funny, but it's also the sort of team building that no staff meeting or practical exercise can accomplish.

Remember, you hired your team because they are experts. When you hired them, you implicitly agreed to trust them. You can be the best leader by allowing them to do their job and lead within their own domain.

It's also important to understand that sometimes when you ask how you can help, the response will be something along the lines of "Thanks, but we've got it under control." That's perfectly acceptable. What's important is that you let it be known that you are available and that you are entrusting your staff to know what's best and what's needed, regardless of what the answer may be.

Over the years, I've often found that simply offering to step in during busy times helps deflate the stress of a situation. Earlier in my career, whenever I heard that a department was crazed or that things were chaotic, I would practically grab my fire hose and sprint down the hall. Nine times out of ten when I arrived to ask what I could do, the answer was "We're good," or I would be asked to do something very small. However, I generally found that just showing up and offering to be of service brought the intensity level down a couple of notches. It let employees know that they weren't going to be left alone to sink or swim. As a result, the stress levels decreased. My team knew I wasn't going to let them fail, so they didn't.

KNOW WHERE TO FIT IN

While you don't have to know everything about everything, you do need to have a good general overview of how things run so you understand where you can be of assistance when the time comes. Generally, this knowledge comes organically when you make a practice of walking around and being aware of what happens outside of your office doors.

You can also be more intentional about acquiring this information. Whenever I start a new position, I make a point of asking every department manager, "What do you expect from me?" or "How can I be of the most help when things get crazy?" Not only does this arm you with information, but it also sets the expectation among staff that your job is to serve them. You let them know that you plan on being present on a day-to-day basis in very real ways.

SCHEDULE TIME TO ROLL UP YOUR SLEEVES

Much as it's important to pitch in when the going gets rough, you also don't want to be the manager who shows up only when there's a fire. You should be intentional about offering to help out during the saner periods as well. In fact, this should be an integral part of your leadership practice. Doing so also offers you a prime opportunity to build out your knowledge base about various departments. Again, sometimes your offer to help won't be accepted, but the offer itself serves as a way to build trust.

One of the first places I would head to was the laundry department. It's so easy to skip the back of the house and focus instead on the front of the house. The back of the house is often known as the heart of the house, and it's true. It's here that you usually find the hardest, most thankless work. These people, almost more than anyone else, deserve your attention.

In the laundry department, I would often go fold towels

and chat. I loved this time and usually folded no more than ten towels. But it meant so much to the team members that they would thank me whenever they ran into me for the remainder of the day.

In Chapter 1, I discussed my practice of walking around the hotel greeting staff for the first two hours of every day. As I made my way through the hotel, I would look for opportunities to help in little ways. For instance, if I was walking through the restaurant to chat with staff in the kitchen and happened to see a table that hadn't been cleared yet, I would bring the dishes back to the dish tank with me. If I walked through the lobby and saw that the pillows needed straightening, I would plump them up. If there was trash lying around, I'd pick it up. Little cues like this that require minimal effort send subtle messages about your role and investment in the team.

As a leader, you are always being watched, whether you are aware of it or not. Most likely, pitching in in small ways isn't going to alter the course of your day in any significant way—but it could have very positive implications over the long run. It will make your staff want to work harder for you. You are walking the walk.

By doing the little jobs that might seem like minutiae, you're also showing each and every employee that what they do is important. It matters. Have you ever thought about the fact that it's generally the lowest-paid individuals at a company who play the largest role in representing and executing your brand?

Let's take Apple, for example. Customers pay approximately $1,000 for a phone. They're not interacting with the six-figure earners who are making and marketing those phones, though. Instead, they see the face of Apple in those frontline employees who make an entry-level hourly wage. Likewise, at multi-million-dollar hotel and restaurant chains, guests aren't interfacing with corporate executives. The person they talk to on the phone or place their order with is likely making minimum wage.

Go down the list of every brand you associate with customer service, and I guarantee you that the person you're actually interacting with—the person who is doing the hard work of representing the brand—is not making a six-figure salary.

More likely than not, you can't change your team members' paychecks. But what you *can* do is make them feel valued and instill in them the confidence that their work is important.

SHOW, DON'T TELL

In this chapter, we've talked at length about sending cues

and messages to employees. This is intentional because part of being a good leader is avoiding telling people what to do to the greatest extent possible. Of course, there are going to be days when you have to ask employees to execute specific tasks. But on a day-to-day basis, this shouldn't be the case. You want to give your employees agency and the opportunity to own their role. When they do this, they will invest in their job, in you, and in the company.

Fostering an environment of service and teamwork is far more effective than doling out orders. You can do this by allowing employees to know you and understand how you operate; in short, you lead by example. This also means that when those moments arrive when you *do* have to ask for specific things to be done, employees will respect you enough to know it's important.

OF COURSE I CAN HELP YOU

One of my favorite memories is when a guest pulled up to the hotel and asked me if I could help him with his bags. Our name tags didn't include job titles, so he had no idea that I was a general manager. I could have told him, "Let me go find a bellman for you," but what was the point? Carrying this guest's bags up to his room was no problem.

"Of course," I responded. And so I did.

When his bags were safely deposited in his room, the guest handed me a $5 bill and asked who the general manager was. "Well, it's me," I told him. The guest looked shocked.

When you think about it, though, this guest really shouldn't have been so shocked. In an ideal customer service environment, the attitude should always be "Of course I can help you!" regardless of job title or the task any team member specifically oversees. This applies equally to management and employees of every level.

IN SUMMARY

The Ritz-Carlton is famous for its motto "We are ladies and gentlemen serving ladies and gentlemen." I go back to this statement over and over again when I think about my role as a leader.

I expect my team members to treat our customers like ladies and gentlemen. Since I expect this of staff, it is nothing short of critical that I treat *them* like ladies and gentlemen. That means I operate on a consistent basis in such a way that the entire team understands that I care, that I value them, and that every single task they do is important enough that I will happily do it myself. With this understanding, team members win and so do the customers they serve.

CHAPTER FIVE

Treat Your Employees like Customers

———

Whenever I take over a new hotel, one of my number one priorities is to upgrade the break room. People look at me funny when I tell them this. "How can *that* be at the top of your list?"

My answer is simple, and it's always the same: "Because it's really important."

Almost across the board, I'm struck by the state of employee-only areas. When leadership thinks about parts of the hotel that need a bit of sprucing up, the break room almost never comes to mind. In reality, there are few areas that are more important to the overall health of the hotel. It's the one place where team members can go for a bit of respite in the midst of taking care of everyone else. They *need* a space that allows them to take a deep breath and relax.

Generally, upgrading the break room doesn't require a huge expense or overhaul (after all, employee break areas rarely take up a lot of space to begin with). However, I do advocate that some money is spent on upgrades and refreshing. When employees aren't on the front lines, they're usually in the break room. You want them to emerge from this space feeling as though they've been replenished and taken care of so that they can pass this feeling along to guests, whether they're in hour one of their shift or hour seven.

Spiffing up break rooms sends a loud and clear message to employees that they matter. It shows them that you are investing in them in a real way. It is a way of treating them like ladies and gentlemen so that they can pay this treatment forward to customers.

For me, break room upgrades generally involve installing new flooring and a fresh coat of paint. I put in a bigger television and make sure the chef understands that there should be a good, fresh meal waiting for team members when they need it. Now, of course, this isn't always possible, depending upon your business.

If your business doesn't have a meal program, there are

other ways to add this benefit through something like a complimentary soda or coffee machine. You can also bring in treats like doughnuts—maybe you can even set up a ritual like Doughnut Day every first Friday or order pizza every now and then. Such actions create a better environment and show team members that you are not just talking the talk but that you're also walking the walk in a way they can't help but notice on a daily basis.

It doesn't stop there. Just as important as fixing up the break room is spending time there. I always make a point of eating with everyone else on staff, which is actually rather unusual. Most managers eat in their office, off-site, or alone and out of sight.

Breaking bread with employees is yet another small, easy way of sending a big message. You are showing rather than just telling employees that you are approachable. You're showing them you're on the same team. And you are cultivating those personal relationships by hanging out in an inherently casual setting that allows employees to speak with you on a one-on-one, peer-to-peer basis. It humanizes you and makes you more than just "the boss."

THE MOP LIST

Just as important as taking care of employees on their downtime is providing them with what they need to complete their role to the best of their ability. As Virgin founder Richard Branson put it, "Your employees are your company's real competitive advantage. They're the ones making the magic happen—so long as their needs are being met."

Every month or so, I would ask the department heads at my hotel, "So, do you have your Mop List?" The idea of the Mop List is taken from a story that is somewhat notorious throughout the hotel industry. It involves employees who became frustrated and disengaged because they were not being provided with the simple things they needed to do their job right. They ended up trying to unionize and, in doing so, brought in a third party. "What are your demands?" this person asked. In the end, all of this strife and discouragement boiled down to the simple fact that a housekeeper who had been there forever needed a new mop, which management refused to provide her with. Clearly, this makes no sense—why not spend $5 so an employee has the tools she needs to succeed?

This might sound crazy, but I assure you it's an experience many employees within the service industry face. I've witnessed housekeepers who literally cry tears of gratitude when I have come into a new hotel and upgraded their vacuum cleaners. While it's great to hear about the gratitude of employees in these situations, providing them with the resources they require to do their job right shouldn't represent a treat or an extenuating circumstance. It should be standard operating procedure.

Obviously, the tools employees need to succeed will sometimes represent a larger expense. However, in my experience, employee requests are usually extremely affordable. I frequently get requests along the lines of more napkins to roll the silverware or two uniform shirts instead of one so that team members don't have to do laundry every night. A small expenditure on your part can make a massive difference in their daily lives. It makes it easier for them to get their job done right, makes them feel like you are invested in their needs, and makes the customers' experience better.

Many managers avoid asking staff about their needs simply because they are aware the business has a limited budget. They don't want to open the door to receiving requests they can't actually fulfill. If you are in this boat, I would encourage you to ask anyway. You will likely be surprised at how simple and low-cost the requests actually are. Also, it's perfectly okay to set the expectation beforehand that you are working within the confines of a set budget. Generally, employees just want what it takes to do their jobs better, and often you are able to facilitate their effort. Everyone wins!

There are always smaller items that have a real impact on

employee satisfaction and productivity. Your willingness to provide them with these tools goes a long way toward communicating their value and your belief in and support of what they are doing.

If you take the time to hire the right people, I firmly believe that employees want to do a good job. They want to provide great service. In order for them to do that, it's up to you to ensure they have the tools they need to follow through. When good employees aren't provided with the tools they need, they begin to grow frustrated and disengaged. Then a couple of things happen: First, service isn't as good as it could be. Second, you begin to lose some of your best employees. Individuals who care about their work and their reputation won't remain at a place where they are being held back from their full potential—nor should they.

Great employees aren't just providing good service for the sake of your company. They're doing it for themselves, too, because it feels good. If you're not going to provide them with what they need to follow through on that aspect of their work, they will ultimately go elsewhere to find a company that will.

If you had a customer who requested something small that would make their experience better, you likely wouldn't hesitate to provide it. Employees should be afforded this same consideration and generosity. Their experience matters just as much as that of your customers—in some ways, perhaps even more so, because your customers' experience is ultimately a direct reflection of your team members' experience.

MANAGE BY WALKING AROUND

Guests love it when they see managers and leaders walking around the facility. I can't even begin to count the number of guests who have said something to me along the lines of "Wow! It's really great to see a general manager in the lobby. You don't see that very often." When you are out and about, it makes you approachable to customers and provides them with an opportunity to give you feedback about both what is working as well as what could be improved to make their experience better.

I was walking around the premises one day shortly after the hotel I was working at put in a club for customers who were part of our loyalty program. As part of this, those customers received a complimentary breakfast. A guest stopped me because he was upset about the plates we provided in the club for the free breakfast. We had put in small plates due to the size of the storage cabinet where they were kept. What we hadn't considered is that customers like the one standing in front of me couldn't put a lot of food on those plates. This particular guest felt like we were trying to prevent our clientele from eating too much food. This thought had never occurred to us.

The next day, we switched out the plates. I never would have found out about this if I hadn't been walking around.

I've also had many guests come up and ask, "Hey, what are you guys doing differently here? Why is everyone so friendly?" To me, this is the ultimate mark of achievement. It means all of these immeasurable and somewhat intangible goals we're striving toward are working.

Another added bonus of managing by walking around is that it sends a subtle cue to team members that you are aware of goings-on in different areas of the business at any given point in time. Rather than having to micromanage to get things done—which no one likes—staff members witness how you behave within the business and can emulate that. Teaching and establishing expectations becomes a more organic and enjoyable process than it might be otherwise. It allows your team to take ownership through observation.

HAVE FUN

Part of any great customer experience is ensuring that they have fun. Like so many other things, this same philosophy should also apply to your team members. Don't get me wrong. Your staff is there to do a job, and obviously, there are plenty of moments when work is just that—work.

Still, add a sense of levity into your working environment when possible. Incorporating fun into work has a direct impact on customers because you are creating a better environment and happier team members. While you can't measure the impact of this effort concretely, you can absolutely see the difference between a workplace that's all business and feels like a drag versus a place where there is room for fun and laughter.

CELEBRATE WINS

An obvious place to infuse fun into your working environment is during those moments when you are celebrating wins with your team. When your employees reach longer-term expectations and goals, acknowledge it. Celebrate it. Use it as an opportunity to have some good old-fashioned fun.

The practice of celebrating wins not only builds your team and makes employees feel appreciated, but it's also a good excuse to set goals. When setting team goals, you want to strive for something that is fairly aggressive but still achievable. Setting goals that are too pie-in-the-sky can potentially be a downer in a case where the team works hard yet still doesn't hit the mark.

I like to set goals around specific milestones. For example, like many other brands, my company performed an annual inspection. In order for a hotel to continue on with the brand, it had to pass that once-over. At the point I came on, the hotel had struggled to pass the inspection on its first try for the past couple of years. Together, my team and I set the goal to pass the initial inspection.

Of course, goals like this are also an expectation, but it's more fun for everyone, and there is more joy in the process when it is accompanied by a celebration once the hard work is done. It's an easy way to incentivize a process.

Celebrations don't necessarily have to be elaborate. In this case, when the team pulled together and passed the inspection on the first try, I went out and bought boxes of Reese's Pieces. I attached a little label to each box that said, "Congratulations on passing the inspection. You're an important *piece* of our team."

Gestures like this aren't the biggest celebration in the world, but they represent a marker and an acknowledgement. There is also a collective sense of victory and pride that comes with pulling together to accomplish a goal.

Much as celebratory gestures with guests don't have to be elaborate or expensive, the same goes with team members. The most important part is acknowledging marker moments with a meaningful gesture, even if it's a small one.

MAKE YOUR OWN OCCASION

All it takes is a quick Google search to realize there is a "national day" for just about anything you can imagine. Embrace it! May 4 is Star Wars Day, so maybe you host a screening or have everyone wear Yoda ears to work. On National Popcorn Day, set up a popcorn machine in the break room. You can multitask with this and bring customers in on the fun too.

You can also designate specific regular events for your team. For example, I'm a big fan of employee pep rallies. Every month, I would set up a one-hour themed pep rally. We would tie the October pep rally into Halloween and have all of the employees dress up. For December, we might have a white elephant gift exchange or breakfast with Santa and invite staff to bring their children in for the occasion. On a more random month, we might have a talent show or set up a karaoke machine. I love doing activities like this because it allows people to show off talents that may not be apparent otherwise, like a beautiful singing voice or a knack for stand-up comedy. In the service sector, there's always a lot of talk about making personal connections, and there is nothing more personal than getting onstage and sharing your talents with your coworkers. These types of activities facilitate the sort of connection and interaction that just isn't possible in the course of a regular workday; they bond teams together and humanize the workplace.

I also like using pep rallies as an opportunity to acknowledge successes, like an employee of the month or a manager of the month. I fill everyone in on relevant rankings, share positive reviews, and make any announcements so that we're all on the same page. If a team member did an outstanding job or achieved some sort of milestone or accomplishment, I will acknowledge that in front of the entire team.

Pep rallies also help alleviate one of employees' most common complaints: that communication is lacking in the workplace and that they're often unaware of what's happening. Monthly gatherings provide an easy solution for this.

Pep rallies might sound cheesy—because, let's be honest, they kind of are—but that doesn't mean they're not effective. I was always surprised by how much employees looked forward to these events. Even when they weren't on the clock, many of them would still show up during their off hours because they didn't want to miss out on the fun and bonding.

IN SUMMARY

The Disney Institute book *Be Our Guest* includes a quote that has always stuck with me: "You can dream, create, design, and build the most wonderful place in the world, but it requires people to make the dream a reality." Bear in mind that this is coming from the masters of customer experience. They go on to say, "It might surprise you, but in our research, people cite the interaction they've had with our cast as the single biggest factor in their satisfaction and intent to return."

That says it all.

Remember, you are investing in your employees. You want them to feel just as valued as your customers because it matters. At the end of the day, your customers are going to remember your employees more than they remember the bed they slept in, the meal they ate, or the product they purchased. It's interactions with your team that will make for memorable customer service. You can directly facilitate this by making your team members' experience with you just as stellar and memorable as the experience you want your guests to have.

PART TWO

Winning Customer-Experience Strategies

CHAPTER SIX

Empower Your People

———

A few years ago, my wife made a reservation at my favorite restaurant, Boca, for my birthday celebration. In the end, she had to cancel the reservation. Several months later, my wife made a different reservation at Boca, this time for a dinner with our family. My wife didn't do or say anything special when she made this second reservation. It was just your normal, run-of-the-mill phone call.

The four of us sat down for dinner that night and ordered our drinks. They were delivered to our table, along with a plate of fried pickles. Note that Boca is a high-end restaurant. They do not serve fried pickles, and we didn't order them. Nonetheless, there was a plate of my all-time favorite comfort food sitting in the center of the table, prepared just how I like them (cut into chips, not spears—this is a critical detail!).

Excited, I look over at my wife. She appeared very confused. It was at this point that our server said to me, "I understand you love fried pickles. These are compliments of the chef." As the server walked away, I leaned over to my wife and thanked her for putting a bug in the chef's ear.

"I didn't!" she responded. "When I made your birthday reservation, I mentioned that fried pickles were your favorite, but that was months ago."

Through this conversation, we realized that Boca obviously has some type of reservation system that allows them to make notes about customer preferences. Not only do they have this system, but they make a point of actively referring to and using it, as the delicious plate of fried pickles sitting on our table proved. We were blown away.

BLOW YOUR CUSTOMERS AWAY

Had the pickle-chip incident happened on my birthday as my wife had originally orchestrated, I still would have been impressed with Boca. However, the fact that it happened months later at the least expected time made it a truly memorable moment. I will forever be loyal to Boca.

Notice that my undying loyalty to this establishment came at virtually no cost to the restaurant. It is also something they never could have accomplished through any amount of marketing or advertising dollars. Intrigued, I started researching the Cincinnati-based Boca Restaurant Group. This led to an interview with CEO and chef David Falk. All told, Boca has more than 650 employees spread throughout restaurants in four different states and continues to grow.

Based on my own experience, I wasn't surprised to learn that Boca has a company-wide philosophy to "blow people away," or as they refer to it, BPA. Falk explains:

> "Our highest ethos in the organization is BPA. It was all predicated on the idea that I was scared to death when I opened my first restaurant because I didn't have anyone to blame for my failure but myself. I just kept saying over and over again, 'We have to blow people away.' Soon, BPA became a noun and a verb. 'We have a BPA on table 77' or 'We BPAed that table.'"

Team members at Boca actively and regularly look for opportunities to blow their customers away. As I can attest, it works!

As Falk shared with me, over the years Boca has even codified the process of blowing people away. It consists of three primary steps:

1. Aggressive listening, which has to be done in a covert way
2. Creative and organic ideas, which have to be genuine and spur-of-the-moment
3. Flawless execution

The idea here is to keep the BPA system as open and flexible as possible. Falk explains, "It nullifies the power if you try to make it too regimented. Genuine hospitality and generosity are really hard to find."

While we are looking at BPA through the lens of the customer in this chapter, it doesn't have to stop there. Falk explains, "My favorite BPAs are when we BPA our staff or our staff BPA each other."

I am personally deeply inspired by this BPA policy, but it's not something most establishments do. Obviously, BPA results in an incredible and memorable customer experience. However, for it to be more than just words on a page, Boca has to do a very important thing: they have to *empower their employees*. To truly blow people away involves more than just polite, rote service. It requires going the extra mile. If team members have to check in with their manager each and every time they want to go that extra mile, it would amount to nothing more than good intentions much of the time.

THE KEYS TO CREATING PERSONAL CONNECTIONS

By empowering your employees, you open the floodgates for unparalleled customer experience. You are essentially handing over the keys to each of your team members, allowing them to create the kind of personal connections and lasting memories that foster a deep-seated loyalty to your brand.

BPA is one way to look at this, but there are plenty of others as well. Marriott, for example, frames this same idea as surprising and delighting guests. They task and entrust each of their team members with finding ways to do exactly that.

Your ultimate goal should be to create a culture in which you completely eliminate the phrase "I need to check with my manager." To create a phenomenal customer service environment, it's critical to remove any barriers that could potentially stand in the way of allowing your employees to do what it takes to make customers happy on a dime.

I've always believed that if you trust your team members, they can do so many things to make your company better—things you would never see or think to do. There are numerous avenues for creativity and attention to detail that could never manifest themselves if it were all left to your single pair of eyes and ears.

As a manager, I make it my goal to *not* know when a customer is upset or frustrated. I aim to create a culture in which every team member understands how I would handle the situation myself and is empowered to take care of it on their own. Of course, I want to know what's happening in my hotel, but a situation in which a customer is already frustrated is only going to be exacerbated if they're asked to hold on while an employee "checks with their manager." To top off their initial frustration, the customer now feels passed on and unheard.

I'm sure you've experienced this feeling before when you've had to call your wireless carrier or cable company only to be passed from one person to the next. Each time you have to retell your story, you end up marinating on what has gone wrong, and as if the initial situation isn't bad enough, even *more* of your time and energy are sucked up as you try to resolve the issue. All too often, this process of sorting out a pain point is more frustrating than the initial incident was to begin with. In the end, even if your issue is resolved, you may very well walk away with a bad taste in your mouth.

I recently had an experience like this in my own life that only served to drive home to me the importance of empowering employees from a customer's point of view. A few months ago, I received a notice from the energy company that they wanted to cut back a tree in my front yard. That's fine. I understood why. However, I couldn't help but notice that this same company had cut down another tree one street over from my house, butchering it down to nothing more than a stump in the process.

The tree that needs to go from my yard just happens to be a beautiful, flowering lily tree that I'm very attached to. I'm okay with this tree being trimmed, but I'm not okay with it being hacked.

So I called the energy company to discuss my concerns. I was told by the customer service representative that she wasn't allowed to give me the phone number or email of the person I needed to speak with. She promised me, however, that she would email this fellow herself.

"Okay, well, can you please copy me on the email?" I asked.

"No," she responded, perfectly politely.

Now, this woman wasn't the first representative I'd spoken with at the company, and she, just like all of the others, was incredibly sweet. Still, it was frustrating even though I understood she simply couldn't help me because her hands were tied due to company policy.

Despite the pleasant demeanor of everyone I was able to speak with at the energy company, I still walked away frustrated. I never heard back from the gentleman I needed to speak with, so I felt unheard. My experience could have been quite different if only the representatives had been empowered to take initiative rather than acting as middlemen in a situation they ultimately had no control of. They missed a prime opportunity to win me over as a loyal customer who felt heard and taken care of.

THE POWER OF TRUST

Inherent in the discussion of empowerment is the fact that you must trust your employees. It is this trust that directly fuels extraordinary customer service. This is precisely why your hiring process is so critical. It's imperative that you hire only people you are willing to trust so that you can empower them to take care of customers without second-guessing their decisions.

Remember, you *hired* your people to do a job. At the end of the day, no matter what specific tasks a team member is responsible for, their primary overarching objective is to take care of customers and earn their loyalty. You cannot expect employees to do this if you are restricting them and putting up a series of hoops for them to jump through in order to do the job you hired them to do.

I'm not advocating for a complete free-for-all, but I *am* saying that you should think of your customer service as a football field. There are out-of-bounds markers that represent anything that involves jeopardizing safety or breaking the law. Aside from that, you need to give your team members free rein of the field to call plays and strategize.

Here's a great example of what those parameters might look like: One of the rules Boca has about BPA is that one customer's great experience can never come at the detriment of another customer's experience. According to Falk, it was this very rule that resulted in what he deems one of the greatest examples of BPA in the company's history.

One evening, a huge Texas college football fan was dining at Boca during a game. She wanted to watch it, but Boca didn't have a TV in the bar or dining room. They did have one in storage, though. Originally, the server considered bringing the television out to the customer's table so she could watch the game while she ate. Then the server realized this might disturb other guests who had come to Boca for a nice, quiet dinner.

The server thought carefully about how he could make his idea work in a way that served everyone's best interests. He struck upon the idea of placing the TV outside a window of the restaurant. He then positioned the drapes so that the football fan had a direct view of the screen, but no one else could see or be distracted by it. Genius.

I always tell my team members that I will support their decisions. The few times that I have felt an employee made a decision I wouldn't have were I to be faced with the same situation, I've responded with a gentle nudge. This might be something along the lines of "Hey, you know what? Next time consider doing X instead." My guess is this will happen rarely, providing you hire and set expectations wisely and diligently. The few times you do have to redirect a team member are worth it. A big part of effective empowerment is instilling in your staff the understanding that you will truly and fully support their decisions.

SERVICE RECOVERY

In a perfect world, your company's product or service would hit the mark 100 percent of the time. Of course, we live in reality, where everything isn't going to go smoothly all of the time, even if you happen to be Apple or Ritz-Carlton.

As a leader, I often feel like I have to be perfect all of the time, even though I know that would be impossible. We are in the business of dealing with humans. With that comes imperfection. You're not going to get it right every time. That's okay. Mistakes can make you better. If you're busy beating yourself up, you might miss that window for growth. Yes, strive for perfection, but also understand that despite your best intentions, sometimes you will miss the mark.

When a glitch happens, you actually have an opportunity. In fact, you should celebrate it because errors provide you with the chance to have an interaction with a guest that you wouldn't normally be able to have.

FIVE STEPS TO SUCCESSFUL SERVICE RECOVERY

I train all of my employees to react to service recovery issues by enacting the LEARN method, a tried-and-true Marriott technique. This model includes five steps that should be used when responding to a guest complaint: listen, empathize, apologize, react, and notify.

Much of the time, all a customer really wants is to be heard, so it's critical to listen to what they are telling you. If you remember, "aggressive listening" is so important that it constitutes one of Boca's three steps to BPA.

Empathy is also important—so important, in fact, that we'll address it as a separate topic later in this chapter. In a nutshell, though, empathy involves putting yourself in the customer's shoes, identifying with their problem, and showing that you genuinely feel their pain.

Apologizing should include something along the lines of

"I'm really sorry that happened, and it's not okay." Own the mistake, even if it had nothing to do with you or if there is some sort of explanation.

React by responding to the issue appropriately. There is no set of rules for reacting; it is entirely dependent upon your team member combining the information they learned from listening with their sense of empathy and cracking the code from there. Let the customer know your intended course of action. When you have completed that, circle back to let the customer know the issue has been taken care of.

Finally, notify anyone necessary so that they are aware of the issue or incident and can prevent it from happening again.

One of the things I love most about the LEARN method is that it can be effectively applied to almost any area of life, including your personal life. I also use LEARN when responding to a team member concern.

Here's what LEARN might look like in practice: Let's say that you manage a restaurant and that a customer tells you their steak is overcooked. You will begin by listening to exactly what they are saying. Let them continue speaking until they have finished. Then and only then do you have the green light to respond. *Do not* talk over them.

It's human nature to want to fix a problem right away. However, in doing this, sometimes you can do more harm than good *if* you haven't let the customer finish whatever it is they want to say. You will have time to react and fix the problem soon, but first you have to listen all the way through.

Empathizing might sound something like "Oh, I like my steak medium-rare too, so I understand how frustrated you are that it's overcooked." Use any personal statement that applies to let the customer know that you understand where they are coming from and that their complaint is valid. Personalizing your response is important because it humanizes the interaction. Remind the guest they're not talking to Acme Restaurant. They're talking to *you*, a human being who can relate to this experience and understand their frustration.

Apologizing is generally pretty straightforward, and it's important to be direct and on the nose. Say, "I'm so sorry. That's not okay. We pride ourselves on making the best steak in the area."

In this situation, the most logical reaction is to let the customer know you will have a new steak made right away. You may also want to comp their entree or give them a free dessert. Read their cues to gauge the appropriate course of action to ensure they walk away feeling good.

Finally, notify whoever is in the kitchen about what has happened. Let them know that the next steak has to be perfect and that this shouldn't happen in the future.

Notice there are no more letters here. There isn't a step that involves the team member speaking to or checking with a manager at any point in this process. By teaching your team members to follow through with the LEARN method, you are empowering them to respond to and resolve customer complaints.

FINESSING SERVICE RECOVERY

A big part of effective service recovery is guaranteeing that the first team member a customer speaks with about an issue is able to resolve it. Initial resolution is perhaps the most important element to customer satisfaction. Everything else can be refined.

One night, a guest checked in only to find that their room key didn't work. The first team member this guest encountered happened to be new on staff. She did exactly what she was supposed to do, which is to hear the guest, take ownership, and resolve the situation. That's precisely what she did—by comping the guest's entire weekend stay.

I found myself at a crossroads. Again, I firmly believe

it's important to support my team members' decisions. However, in this instance, a free weekend stay seemed excessive. Still, I had empowered this employee, and particularly since she was new, I didn't want to set up a scenario where she never felt comfortable performing service recovery again.

In this case, I decided to address the matter by sitting this woman down and praising her for making sure the guest was happy. I then helped her understand that in the future, while she should certainly do what she felt was necessary, something along the lines of a free breakfast might suffice.

With this—and *especially* in terms of service recovery—I'm not suggesting that there is any sort of prescriptive advice or formula I can offer to equate X problem with X solution. In fact, I am adamantly against that practice. As a testament to this, I recently went into the back office of a hotel and tore a chart off the wall that linked specific guest complaints to specific solutions. (For example, if a guest complains that a light bulb is out, offer them free breakfast.)

The problem with being formulaic about service recovery is that everyone's perception of a given problem is so different. Going back to the example of the room key, I happened to be around when this situation went down, so I knew for a fact that the guest wasn't too upset about it. However, I have also seen guests get extremely worked up in the exact same scenario. So in their case, a free weekend might be exactly what it takes to alleviate the situation. It all works on a case-by-case basis that should take into account how frustrated the guest is and the issue at hand. Let your customer show you what the appropriate response to a situation is.

EMPATHY

A great customer service representative will seek to understand the person standing in front of them rather than the black-and-white facts of a situation. A prescriptive chart or formula will never be able to take into account what a guest is dealing with on a personal level or what they happened to have encountered in life before the incident occurred. For example, if a guest is staying at my hotel immediately following his mother's funeral and his room key doesn't work, it makes sense that he could be quite upset about the situation. Rightly so.

We deal with humans, so all of these very intangible and unpredictable factors matter. You want your team members to be able to read people and make decisions based on what they see. This is an art, not a science.

Whether you recover from a service glitch by offering free

meals for life or a slice of cake on the house isn't really important. What does matter is that your team members respond with empathy. If you can be empathetic, demonstrate that you genuinely understand why a guest is upset, and acknowledge and own the situation, you will likely not only come out of the situation A-OK but, more often than not, much better off than you would have been had the situation not occurred in the first place.

This means that a customer will likely respond quite differently to a response like "I'll take care of everything" versus "It is not okay that this happened. That is not what we're known for, nor is it how we do business. I am sorry this happened, and here is what I'm going to do." The first response is just an action; the second response expresses understanding, acknowledgment, ownership, and empathy. It is humanizing. It is connection. If you put yourself in the customer's shoes, you can clearly see why the second option is so much more effective than the first.

THE COST OF EMPOWERMENT

It also bears mentioning that, in most cases, empathy is enough. Usually, a guest just wants to feel heard. It is your job to do that. Further expense is generally not required. For example, if I buy a pair of jeans only to go home and realize they are damaged, I want the jeans replaced or refunded in a courteous manner. This comes at no additional expense to the company.

This is important to understand in order to alleviate the common fear managers have that giving the reins to the frontline staff will represent a major expense—a fear I've literally never seen materialize. I've also never spoken with anyone who has seen this be the case. Yes, there may be an occasional scenario when someone requires a complete refund. However, this type of situation is very much the exception and not the rule, and it ultimately boils down to a minor expense in return for a huge payoff.

The alternative, on the other hand, will cost you a lot. If a customer feels unheard and expresses that in the form of a negative review or word of mouth, you can lose not only a lot of money but also a lot of positive buzz and potential customer loyalty. This directly translates to a loss in income. In fact, according to a recent report by Accenture, $1.6 trillion per year is lost by companies in the United States due to customers lost as a result of poor customer service.

TURNING BAD REVIEWS INTO A WIN

It's not just reviews that matter but also how you *respond* to reviews, especially negative reviews.

Everyone gets a negative review now and then. When that happens to you, don't ignore it or battle it out. You will always look bad. Instead, thank the customer for their feedback. Keep it brief, and offer your contact information for further communication.

Also, remember that, at this point, most people are aware that some reviewers are just angry. If you have a page full of positive reviews and one angry customer who you respond to politely, most readers will understand what is actually going on here. Not only that, but you can actually win points by dealing with reviews in a straightforward, diplomatic manner.

Most great managers and companies understand the value of giving something away to make someone happy. Rarely is drawing a line in the sand worth it because you will pay so much more for it down the road in terms of negative publicity or social reviews. The bottom line is that in today's environment, that's how people are choosing where to spend their dollars.

Your future customers are making their spending decisions based on the previous experiences of other people. They choose the hotel they'll stay at based on TripAdvisor reviews, they choose where to have dinner based on Yelp, and they choose their service providers based on Angie's List. You can make a pretty compelling argument that, at this point, reviews are worth way more than advertising dollars.

MAKING MEANINGFUL CONNECTIONS

One of the biggest contributors to generating customer loyalty is finding ways to make a lasting, meaningful connection with them. This can be as simple as looking for and responding to cues.

In the hotel industry, for example, a simple, straightforward cue is a family traveling with children. Traveling with children can be a challenge, which is compounded by the fact that many establishments aren't very welcoming of kids. I always encourage my team members to stay on the lookout for families and go out of their way to let them know that we're glad they have joined us and want them to be comfortable throughout their stay. This is a small gesture that goes a long way and seems to mean a lot to customers.

You can take this even further. If your hotel has a pool, consider ordering beach balls with the hotel logo on them and distributing them to little kids at check-in. This immediately signals not only that are you okay with having children at your hotel but that you welcome them. You might also share some tips about great local attractions for kids.

I once worked at a hotel that was close to a children's hospital, so we often had patients stay with us. Our staff was acutely aware of this. Whenever they spotted a patient, they would bend over backward to take care of the child and family. Sometimes they would even go so far as to run out to buy the child a toy and send it to their room with a card.

If you see kids at a table in a restaurant, bring them a snack while they wait or serve their meal early. There are any number of cues your team members might catch on to and can act upon in a variety of ways.

Also, remember this simple fact when it comes to making a connection: There is nothing more personal than using a customer's name. If they're filling out a form or signing a credit card receipt, note their name and use it. In the absence of this, always feel free to ask their name. It's a really small thing that goes a very long way.

You might be seeing a theme here: as with so many other aspects we've discussed throughout this book, you don't have to respond in big, elaborate, or costly ways. The biggest thing is to recognize cues and let the customer know that you see them and are invested in their well-being. Encourage your staff to take the time to read customers and to actively seek out these moments.

I have seen so many incredible and heartwarming examples of this from various team members over the years. My favorite thing is when I find out about these little moments after the fact. I had no idea they were even happening and was never asked for permission or support, even on those occasions when they did involve some expenditure—a sign of truly empowered employees who are living and breathing the customer service culture.

Even better than that are the times when I never hear about these moments at all from the staff. Instead, I receive a call or email from a previous guest at some point down the line, reaching out to let me know that our staff made a positive impact.

IN SUMMARY

A customer's perception of your company is usually made in little moments. You want to ensure that your business is providing as many of these moments as possible and that they are as organic as possible. The scope of such an accomplishment is far beyond what any single person can possibly do. So it is essential that you empower your employees to take action. That is how these memorable moments are made and how customers develop a deep and lasting connection with your business. Make it your goal to never again have a team member say, "Sure, but I just have to check with my manager first."

CHAPTER SEVEN

Everything Speaks

I am fanatical about doormats. I want them to be perfectly straight and impeccably clean. I'm constantly straightening them out and brushing them off. It might make me seem a bit quirky at times, but there's a good reason for my obsession.

Your customer's first impression of your business happens way before they even walk through your front door or come into contact with one of your staff members. No matter how beautiful and well-kept your hotel, restaurant, or salon is, if your parking lot is riddled with potholes, customers will notice that. If there are weeds in the flower beds leading up to your entrance, clients will see them. And of course, if your doormat is dirty and askew, people are going to look down at your logo and make an association, subconscious though it may be.

In truth, customers are forming an impression of your brand even before *that*. They begin formulating their opinions about you when they land on a review or your website or social media page. Does the imagery communicate what you're trying to say? Does your page load properly? Perhaps you've noticed this. Whereas the initial web page image of a service establishment used to be a picture of the building, now it tends to be a close-up detail shot of an item such as a cocktail or beach chair. That's because businesses are realizing that more important than sharing a literal image is conveying the *feeling* they want customers to have when they visit an establishment.

Doormats matter, just like every other seemingly innocuous element of your business matters. Customers notice these things because everything speaks, down to the littlest detail.

THE CUSTOMER JOURNEY

When I consult with clients, one of the first things I recommend they do is plot out a customer journey map. The purpose of this map is to put on paper a visual representation of the journey a customer takes through your business from beginning to end. The goal of the journey map is to help everyone in your organization step in to the shoes of your customer. You want each team member to have a specific, detailed understanding of what the customer will experience during their time with you. It also helps employees understand where they fit into the larger process. The map is a visual representation that allows your staff to see how their interaction builds and contributes to the entire experience of the customer. It allows each team member to see that their interaction is an integral part of the customer's overall journey through the business.

Creating this map is fairly straightforward. The most important part of the process is paying attention to and thinking through every single step the customer will take in the course of doing business with you.

For example, if I were drawing out a customer journey map to illustrate a customer's overall experience at a hotel, it might look like this. First, the customer will see an advertisement or hear about the hotel from a previous customer. From there, they might visit the website or call the hotel to make a reservation. They receive an email confirmation, show up at the hotel, check in at the front desk, go to their room, utilize the products and services both in their room and in the hotel, and walk around different points of the property. Finally, the customer checks out, receives an email or a receipt, and then perhaps goes online to review the business. Each of these elements represents a specific point on the journey map.

Customers form their opinion about your company as a whole. Sure, they might have a great experience booking their reservation, interacting with an associate at the front desk, and sleeping in a soft, cozy bed. But if they go to breakfast the next morning and have a waiter with a bad attitude and are served cold, runny eggs, suddenly the whole experience is tainted.

This might seem a little ridiculous. After all, why let one bad breakfast leave a bad taste in your mouth about the entire stay, which was otherwise impeccable? Well, unfortunately this is human nature. In fact, according to a 2012 *New York Times* article entitled "Praise Is Fleeting, but Brickbats We Recall," author and Stanford University professor Clifford Nass explains:

> Almost everyone remembers negative things more strongly and in more detail. The brain handles positive and negative information in different hemispheres. Negative emotions generally involve more thinking, and the information is processed more thoroughly than positive ones. Thus, we tend to ruminate more about unpleasant events—and use stronger words to describe them—than happy ones.

The same article goes on to say that it takes a ratio of five good events to overcome every bad one. To mitigate this, you want every team member along the way to be aligned with your customer service culture and to understand how they impact the big picture. You want them to think about the little details.

CREATE A MULTISENSORY EXPERIENCE

My philosophy that "everything speaks" was inspired by the Disney book I mentioned previously, *Be Our Guest*. This book discusses how every single element of your establishment directly speaks to your guests. The idea is summarized like this:

> In Disney theme parks, 'everything speaks' means that every detail from the doorknobs to the dining room sends a message to the guest. The message must be consistent with the common purpose and quality standards, and it must support and further the show being created. The next time you're in the Magic Kingdom, have fun and pay attention to what your feet sense as you walk from one themed area to the next. Setting includes the environment, the objects located with the environment, and the procedures that enhance the quality of the environment.

While we're not all running multi-billion-dollar corporations, this advice applies equally to any business in the service industry. Although you're likely not aiming to create your own fantastical world within your establishment, you do still want the customer's experience to be immersive. One way to do this is by appealing to the senses.

Perhaps you've noticed over the past several years that there has been an increased emphasis on multisensory experiences. For instance, most hotel brands now have their own scent, which is pumped into the building behind the scenes. A lot of them even sell candles of that scent in their gift shop. This scent might be evocative of relaxation, luxury, or any number of other sensations that you want guests to associate with your establishment.

Along with scent, brands are now also relying more on music and lighting to set the mood. For example, in the morning, the lighting might be brighter, and they might play upbeat music with fewer lyrics. As the day goes by and the evening draws near, the lighting will begin to come down, and the music will become a bit more poppy, with more lyrics incorporated.

Smell, sound, and light all help create not only a sense of arrival but also a sense of place. It's a way to express your identity and make yourself memorable to guests. It's how you create a richer experience for them. At some hotels, you might find that the nighttime vibe in the lobby is more similar to a club than a hotel. That is a very specific choice, likely with the aim of encouraging guests to stick around and have a cocktail in the bar rather than going straight up to their room.

This same sentiment should apply to all areas of your

business. Take the time to walk around and see where and how you can infuse intentional details throughout. Use that journey map, and guide yourself through the customer experience by seeing, smelling, and hearing the environment as they would.

The other nice thing about appealing to your customers' senses is that it doesn't involve much expense or heavy lifting. Cumulatively, though, the effect is fairly significant. Start with your music and lighting. Make sure the music you are playing isn't dependent upon Pandora's or Spotify's whims. Be intentional and consistent, using music as an integral part of the tone you want to establish and the experience you want customers to have. Similarly, the lighting is easy to incorporate. What settings play into the vibe you want to set for customers? Bright and cheery, or dim and moody? Or perhaps you want to switch your lighting up, depending upon the time of day. Again, come back to those ideas of intention and consistency.

IT'S ALL IN THE DETAILS

Pay attention to other cues you're sending as well. I recently went to a restaurant and used the restroom before ordering. It was disgusting—the kind of disgusting that makes you want to cover your hand with something before touching the doorknob. Despite the fact that the dining room was perfectly clean, I still walked out. That one element of the restaurant conveyed a loud message to me that this was not a place that was invested in cleanliness. The meal likely would have tasted perfectly good, but nonetheless, my experience was ruined by a detail. I never even made it to the main attraction, which is, of course, the food.

While this experience was relatively extreme, you can inadvertently have a similar impact on guests in much smaller, more innocuous ways. Think about how your impression of a business changes over time. Your first impression tends to be pretty global. You might think, "Wow, this place is incredible! Everything is perfect." Then you spend more time there and begin to notice details that weren't apparent at first glance. For instance, maybe you sit down and notice the furniture or carpet is worn. Once you're aware of this detail, you begin looking a bit closer and spot a couple of dust bunnies. Added up, these little things begin to detract from your overall experience.

Sometimes, it's difficult to see a place you are familiar with through a fresh set of eyes. This is why it can be a good idea to bring in someone who is unfamiliar with your business to get some honest, straightforward feedback. This might be as simple as asking a friend to come have dinner at your restaurant on the house in exchange for sharing their take on the details of the experience.

You can think of it as having your own personal mystery shopper.

As you refine the details of your business, remember that they extend beyond just the physical elements of your establishment. How your employees look conveys a clear message to customers as well. How are they dressed? Are they well groomed? Do they look sharp and professional? If your customer sees a server who is in uniform but their shirt is half-untucked, their apron is dirty, and their hair is disheveled, it's probably going to impact how the customer perceives their service experience, even if all of the other elements are in place.

Most, if not all, companies have uniform or dress code standards and guidelines in place. When a staff member doesn't follow these guidelines, make sure you reinforce them. Honestly, this probably isn't one of the more fun parts of your job. Don't be demeaning about it, of course, but do address the situation when necessary. Make your life easier by establishing that expectation from the get-go.

Finally, as you are examining the details of your establishment, keep an eye out for one of the disruptive elements that I see most frequently: signage. All too often, service industry businesses have negative signage up that they are so accustomed to that they don't even notice it anymore. I'm talking about things like your standard "No shoes, no shirt, no service" sign. Is that really necessary? Probably not. It's a small thing, but it can plant the seed of poor customer service in a patron's mind.

This leads me to one of my biggest pet peeves: handwritten signs. If something is out of order and temporarily unusable, that's fine. It happens. But in this case, type—don't handwrite—a sign that is neat and correctly written. Include an apology along the lines of "Sorry for the inconvenience" and provide any additional information necessary. Even in an instance when something isn't working, you want to keep the emphasis on what *is* available and what you *can* do, as opposed to what you can't. For example, if a vending machine is broken, include details about where customers can find another vending machine close by.

Be sure to check for signage in the back of the house as well. I'm talking about policy statements in bold type and other signs of this variety. I've seen signs that say "Complaint free" followed by a blank space next to the word "days." Underneath, it says, "Get a manager with any issue." *No.* This is negative messaging. You are communicating to employees (and worse, any customer who happens to see it) that, first of all, you expect complaints. Second of all, you already know how I feel about getting managers. Signs like this—even when their intention is to convey policy—set up the framework for your customer to have a bad experience.

IN SUMMARY

You are building an experience for your customer, and every single detail contributes to that experience, for better or for worse. If you're serious about creating well-rounded, exceptional service, I encourage you not just to pay attention to detail but to pay fanatical attention to detail.

If a guest walks into an area or has an experience that isn't consistent with the rest of the establishment, it can detract from the entire experience in both big and small ways.

Check your doormats.

CHAPTER EIGHT

Aggressive Hospitality

Most hotels are actually two hotels. They are one hotel between Sunday and Thursday, and a completely different entity on Friday and Saturday. Sunday through Thursday, hotels tend to appeal mainly to corporate customers; on the weekends, they cater to more laid-back vacationing customers and families.

I once worked at a hotel that had many children's athletic teams come through on the weekends. The truth is that many people on our staff dreaded weekends because of this. There were so many kids on-site that they would overtake the hotel. Because they—and often the parents traveling with them—weren't seasoned travelers, their expectations were different than those of our more experienced guests. They tended to require more attention, which strained the staff.

The collateral impact wasn't only a decline in customer service, but also in employee performance in general. Team members would call in sick on the weekend days, and even if customers weren't specifically aware of what was happening, there is no doubt they could feel it. As a result, the same hotel that would get rave reviews during the week from corporate customers didn't fare so well on the weekends. More than once, I was told by a customer, "It's clear we weren't wanted." This commentary applied to the exact same staff who had won over corporate clients during the weekdays.

I knew something had to change, so I gathered the leadership team together to brainstorm. Within that group, there were a couple of soccer moms and dads who spoke to their experience of traveling with kids and, specifically, with teams of kids. They filled us all in on what their dream hotel scenario would look like.

Based on this feedback, we came up with a set of standard operating procedures to be implemented specifically on the weekends for our athletic team guests. By now, you probably won't be surprised to hear that all of these measures were small and either cost-effective or cost-free.

We put two coolers of ice at the front entrance and made signs that read, "Welcome! We're glad you're here. Free ice. Enjoy the weekend!" and "Good luck this weekend!" With this, before guests even arrived at the front desk, they were already feeling welcome and taken care of in ways they had never seen at a hotel before. This benefitted us, too, because usually these teams drained our ice machines to fill up their coolers, which meant there was no ice left for other guests.

Speaking of the front desk, like most hotels, we have a list of policies. These are particularly important during the weekend because of the 10:00 p.m. curfew to ensure guests can sleep. The problem is that, first of all, "policy" is a dirty, non-service-oriented word. Instead of saying, "Hey, we're glad you're here," policies say, "Hey, here are our rules." Not the best way to start off a weekend of carefree fun.

To resolve this, we reformatted this list into a brochure. The front cover said, "Welcome," and we inserted the guest's team logo underneath that to personalize the document. This brochure included our rules and policies, but it included a lot of other things too. The interior of the brochure highlighted things we were going to do for our guests over the course of the weekend. This included little treats like cookies and milk in the lobby on Friday night and ice cream on Saturday.

We also let them know that we would wash their uniforms overnight so they would be clean for the next day's game. This was designed to alleviate the fact that we often saw parents sitting by the public washer and dryer until midnight, taking care of this chore themselves. Laundry always spiraled into a whole set of other issues: parents were cranky from washing clothes till the wee hours, they were annoyed that we had only one washer and dryer (because they were never used on the other days of the week), and other guests were annoyed by the noise. A quick fix resolved all these problems: we realized we could use our commercial washer and dryer that sat empty all night anyway. This process took all of fifteen minutes on our end. Let me tell you, guests ate this up. And we won too!

We also included a listing of fun local things to do, places to go, and restaurants to visit on their off time. On rainy days, we would offer them the use of one of our meeting rooms to order pizza. The setup was great for them, and it also kept the kids from running around our halls at night. On their last day, we would give every team member a Gatorade on their way to the game.

That's it. All very simple actions! Never again did I hear that our weekend guests didn't feel welcome. In fact, we started receiving glowing reviews from our athletic-team visitors. On the employee side, things were much better too. Staff stopped calling in sick because they weren't getting bombarded with complaints. Our guests were happy, so our employees were happy and vice versa.

THINK OUTSIDE THE BOX

All we did in the example of the traveling youth sports teams was think outside the box a little bit. I've found that in this and other scenarios, these types of creative solutions not only solve the problem at hand but offer other unforeseen benefits as well. For example, what we didn't anticipate was that our bar revenue would increase with these procedural changes. However, it did because all of those guests who used to sit by the washing machine at night now had the free time to unwind and have a cocktail and appetizer.

Often, this goes back to that idea of BPA. We don't usually associate the word "aggressive" with "hospitality," but there is an element of aggression to it. You want your staff to be aggressive in their ability to look for—and then act upon—ways to impact your customers' experience that might not be immediately apparent or that are somehow out of the ordinary. The idea of aggressive hospitality occurred to me when I saw my first general manager be almost like a bull in a china shop while greeting customers in the lobby. He was everywhere you looked, always asking how a customer was and what he could do to help.

There was passion behind what he did, and that passion was immediately apparent to customers and team members alike. He let customers know, in no uncertain terms, that he was there to take care of them. Without using the specific words, he let them know in a crystal clear way that not only was hospitality his job, but it was also what he loved and really wanted to do.

Aggressive hospitality might look like this: a customer arrives at the front desk soaking wet after just having run through the rain. The attendant notices and, without asking, hands the customer a towel. Or maybe a customer sets an empty bottle of water down on the counter while signing their credit card bill. In response, your attendant takes the old bottle and replaces it with a new one. It's one thing to just offer to take the old water bottle off their hands; it's next-level to replace it with a fresh one.

It doesn't take much to let people know you appreciate the fact that they are spending their time with you. However, the payoff is huge.

THE 15/5 RULE

The 15/5 rule is one of the cornerstones of aggressive hospitality and an expectation I always set with our team. The way it works is that employees should make eye contact and smile at any guest within fifteen feet of them.

Within five feet, a pleasant verbal exchange should be initiated—just something simple along the lines of "Good morning" or "How are you?"

I know this sounds super simple on the surface. And in fact, it *is* super simple, but that doesn't mean it's the norm. How many times have you walked by an employee at a business you're paying money to without them acknowledging you? It's awkward, and it happens a lot. Which is kind of good news for you because it allows your customer service experience to stand out that much more.

Also, by initiating conversation, employees are giving customers an opening to engage more so that they have the opportunity to glean those tidbits that can be put toward cultivating an outstanding customer experience. Customers always ask me, "Why is everyone so friendly here?" I would guess that the 15/5 rule greatly contributes to this perception.

REWARD LOYALTY

All of your customers are equally important. However, you do want to be able to distinguish who your most loyal customers are and to acknowledge them. This is a particularly great set of people to look for ways to wow, especially because you probably know more personal information about them due to the sheer volume of their business and your interactions with them. To be clear, this doesn't mean they should receive better service than anyone else. After all, it's great service with customers of all stripes that will ultimately generate that loyalty. However, regular customers do offer more opportunities for memorable interactions.

Many larger companies and brands have built-in rewards programs. These are great, but they're not necessarily personal. At one hotel I worked at, I would personally write platinum guests (customers who spent seventy-five nights with the brand) an email. It usually read something like this:

Dear Sam,

I really appreciate your loyalty. Thank you for staying with us.

My name is Ryan. I'm the general manager. If there's any way that we can make your stays more enjoyable, please let me know.

Thank you for your loyalty,

Ryan

Simple, right? Yet I can't tell you how many responses

I got from people saying something along the lines of "Wow, I never receive personal communication like this. Thank you." This type of interaction also opens up the door to the possibilities of additional memorable interactions because they can proactively reach out to you in the future.

Here's a great example: Sam stayed with us every week. He was in the process of relocating to the area, so on one occasion, he brought his family to stay with him for the weekend. He emailed me before his stay to ask if I could make sure he got two beds for that trip.

Yes! A prime opportunity! Instead of two beds, I gave him two connecting rooms and comped one of them. It was a slow weekend, and that second room was going to be empty anyway. It's such an easy thing for us to do. Sam checked in and looked like a rock star in front of his family. He was happy, and so was I. In fact, Sam was so thrilled that he moved all of his company business to our property.

YOUR CUSTOMERS HAVE EXPECTATIONS TOO

Just like you have expectations of your staff, your customers have a set of expectations of your business. These might be different from one guest to the next. So how do you ever crack the code on what a customer wants?

You must be able to understand where a customer is coming from.

You can do this in two ways: first, by listening to what customers are asking about or looking for on a literal level. If a customer asks for something, go out of your way to accommodate them, even if that request is off the beaten track. Second, as we discussed earlier, you need to be able to read your customers.

Your customers are going to come to you in all states, and you should never make assumptions. I can't tell you how many times I've checked in a guest and asked what brought them to town only to be told, "I'm here for a funeral." When you receive this or any other answer, at this point you can begin to anticipate what they might need given the circumstances or what might make them more comfortable. What would you want if you were in their shoes? This is always the best place to start.

You can anticipate needs in more general ways too. If rain is in the forecast, put out umbrellas for customers to grab. If you see a customer leave to go for a run, be ready and waiting for their return with a bottle of water and a towel on hand. If you notice a customer is dining alone, make a point of positioning them so they face a window or television and drop off a magazine or newspaper. Offer a complimentary beverage in your waiting area. These little things communicate a high level of service.

Not only do customers love these gestures, but it also feels good to be the person who provides that little slice of happiness or surprise. A service-oriented employee will get excited every time they see a window of opportunity in this vein. There aren't always a lot of chances in life to proactively be the bit of sunshine in someone's day. Service employees have that chance on a more regular basis than most people, and if your staff is on the lookout for these inroads, they'll find a lot of them.

BECOME A PART OF THE STORY

When you find little, personalized inroads to add to a customer's experience, you're giving them a story to tell, and who doesn't love to tell a story? All the better if that story involves you and how outstanding and special your establishment is. If you offer good service, well, yeah, that's great. But are customers going to share that with others in the form of a story? Probably not.

You become a part of the customer's story by leveling up your service to the point where it becomes memorable. One of my favorite examples of this happened when I worked at an airport hotel. A family came to us, stranded because of a flight cancellation. There were six people in the family, and the only room we had available had just one king-size bed.

We could have just figured, "Well, at least they have a place to stay," and that would have been the end of that. Most likely, the family still would have been satisfied because at least they weren't sleeping in the terminal.

In this case, one of my employees decided to make an adventure out of it for the family. He went to the housekeeping closet, got a bunch of extra blankets and pillows, hunted down some coloring books, and collected some snacks from the kitchen. He brought all of this up to the room and told the kids they got to have a sleepover. He even went so far as to create makeshift beds for them on the floor.

The parents were blown away—so much so, in fact, that they wrote a handwritten letter expressing their gratitude and amazement. What had been a really stressful night turned into a fun, unexpected adventure. They'll probably tell this story forever.

IN SUMMARY

Customer service is an active pursuit. At any given moment, you and your staff should be on the lookout for the opportunity to make your customers feel not only welcome, but also special. Go ahead: blow them away.

.

Conclusion

No matter what kind of business you work in, if you are customer-facing, you always have the opportunity to be aggressively hospitable in ways that will thrill your clients. I was recently on the receiving end of this, and it reminded me, yet again, why all of the elements we've discussed in this book are so important.

I went to CVS to pick up a prescription for my wife. Because she recently changed jobs, they didn't have her insurance information. The end result of this was a prescription she needed that cost hundreds of dollars. I was taken aback, to say the least. Not to mention that I was incredibly frustrated.

The clerk told me that they would try to figure the situation out but that it would take a couple of days. When I called my wife to tell her what was going on, I didn't notice that a pharmacist was walking down the aisle where I was standing. I hung up the phone, and he approached me. "Is everything okay?" he asked.

"I'm fine," I told him. "It's just that our insurance hasn't come through, and I need to pick up a prescription."

"Well, is there any way I can help?" he asked.

"I don't think so," I shrugged.

Undeterred, he said, "Let me try."

The pharmacist walked me up to the counter, asked my name, and introduced himself. I explained the whole situation. He looked up the prescription my wife needed and explained that the reason it was so expensive was because we got the prescription for a month at a time. He advised me to get the prescription in smaller increments and let me know there were coupons online that would bring the price down. He gave me the web address, entered the prescription I was looking for onto my phone, and pulled up a coupon so that my wife could get the prescription free for a week. The pharmacist ended our interaction by thanking *me*, despite the fact that he was the person who had done all of the work.

In the end, the pharmacist spent several minutes with

me. It blew me away. There was no reason for him to do this, but he did, and it was so impactful. I mean, I don't know about you, but I don't normally think of pharmacists as customer service champions. This guy was, and he earned his pharmacy my and my wife's loyalty forever.

He gave me a really good story.

Acknowledgments

———

This section could go on for pages because I could thank each and every person I've worked with for something specific and meaningful. To the thousands of team members I've worked with over the years: You've sacrificed time with your family, and missed holidays and special events for the sake of our team. Not only that, but you have contributed to my growth both as a leader and as a person. I am so grateful to each and every one of you. Thank you for coming in every day.

I am grateful to Brian Perkins, who gave me my first job as a front desk manager despite the fact that I had no hotel experience. He helped me discover my love of hospitality as well as modeled what a good leader looks like. As far as first bosses go, they don't get much better than Brian.

A big thank you to Mark David Jones, who has been both an inspiration and an incredible source of information.

To Joe Hinson and the fine folks at the West Chester Liberty Chamber Alliance and Mark Hecquet at the Butler County Visitors Bureau, I am so appreciative of your constant support and encouragement.

To my wife, Geetha, who can see what lights me up in ways that even I cannot. She is the engine that drives me to follow my dreams and make things happen.

And of course, thank you to Rosie, who has been by my side for the entire time I have written this book. Rosie, you are the best dog a guy could ever wish for.

About the Author

 **CHARLES RYAN MINTON** is a customer service expert, a keynote speaker, and the president of CRM Hospitality & Consulting, LLC. An award-winning former hotel general manager for some of the world's biggest brands, Ryan has helped shape the customer service experiences of high-profile companies such as Jaguar, Land Rover, Hilton Hotels Worldwide, Marriott International, InterContinental Hotels Group, Gannett, Ultimate Jet Charters, and Delaware North.

Ryan speaks at conferences, workshops, and company meetings worldwide. He works with companies of all sizes and across all service industries. Visit him at CharlesRyanMinton.com.